I FELL IN LOVE WITH A MAN WHO DIDN'T EXIST

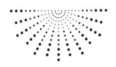

LOVINA STARR

The names and details in this book, including my own, have been changed in order to maintain the dignity and privacy of others.

This book, the first of many, reflects the earlier years of my life, between the ages of 26 and 31 years young, and my experiences with narcissism, alcoholism and addictive personalities.

CONTENTS

INTRODUCTION

Narcissism is empathy's evil twin. The name originates from the myth about a handsome Greek youth called Narcissus, who rejected the advances of the nymph Echo. In doing so, Narcissus fell in love with his own reflection, seen within a pool of water. In later years, psychiatrists started to use the term narcissism to describe a mental condition in which people have an inflated sense of their own importance and a deep need for excessive attention and admiration. Sigmund Freud, the founder of psychoanalysis, said that narcissism is a normal stage within child development, but when it appears or occurs post puberty it should be considered a disorder. Now, the word narcissism seems to be part of everyday language. When did the shift happen to make Narcissistic Personality Disorder (or NPD, as it is known for short) a modern-day buzz term? After all, it is a serious mental health disorder that can detrimentally affect the lives and wellbeing of both the sufferer and those around them.

So, how did I come to write a book about narcissism? First, it comes from my drive to help people. I run my own life coaching business, and I aim to treat anyone who needs to find stability in their lives, whether physically, mentally, emotionally or spiritually – or all four. I can go from helping people to live without pain, to showing them how to achieve a balanced state of mind. I try to bring an aura of positivity and dedication to everything that I do, and I am passionate about working with people to eliminate any stress and anxiety that may be preventing them from enjoying their life to the fullest, thereby allowing them to become the best version of themselves. Following the loss of my mother, along with other personal tragedies and my reactions to them, I decided that I would never preach to or judge another. I strive to continuously develop, learn and grow. Additionally, having worked with clients in a co-dependent relationship with a narcissist, and having my own experience of being in one, I decided to put pen to paper and write my memoirs. They can be used as a tool to help you find your own route to long-lasting health and happiness. Ultimately, health and happiness come from knowing who you are and loving yourself from the inside out. Self-love plays such a huge role in the life of a balanced person. I teach my clients to use it to live their life as though all their dreams have come true, and then to challenge their reality to catch up.

I fell in love with a narcissist, and had I not had a strong sense of self, it could have destroyed me. I can honestly and authentically identify with many of you reading this, who are either with or have been with a narcissist. Perhaps you have picked this book up because you are worried that you may be in love with one, or simply because you were drawn to the book's title. Whatever your motivation, I firmly believe that everything happens for a reason. I sincerely hope and pray that these memoirs either help you or enable you to help others.

I am not a psychotherapist, so I don't have the credentials to diagnose a narcissist. However, I can help you to spot one. First of all, a narcissist will display an arrogant attitude and haughty behaviour. They will reveal themselves to be a person who truly believes they are special and unique. They will require excessive admiration, and they will not tolerate your focus being shifted from them to others within their circle of trust. For example, they might envy attention given to their children. People around the narcissist may rightly think that what they are doing is hurtful, but the narcissist won't care as long as it means their own needs are being met.

I believe that today's social media selfie culture encourages narcissistic tendencies, and while it's difficult to say whether narcissism is on the rise, I wouldn't be surprised to see an increase in NPD diagnoses within the next decade or so. I observe social media platforms on a daily basis, and I am aware that 'narc spotting' has become a bit of a sport.

Empathy, compassion, love, hope and joy are the traits that make us human. I feel that we need to shift back to understanding 'the self'. In order for humanity to be at its best, we need to comprehend why we do what we do and then choose kindness. However, narcissists cannot identify with 'the self' or with the concept of giving selflessly. My concern is that our world will soon be filled with an abundance of people lacking empathy, kindness and a 'selfless' heart.

I believe that with the right help, narcissists can heal themselves enough to lead a better life, and to be the best version of themselves, without hurting others. As the saying goes, "Great oaks from little acorns grow." So, from starting small, we can collectively shift away from a narcissistic world towards a more joyous, compassionate and empathetic one. I pray that the time spent writing and producing this book will serve Jesus, and that it will not be in vain. After all, I was strongly guided by Him to write my memoirs, in order to help others with their self-healing and learn how to love the broken unconditionally.

ROSE-TINTED GLASSES

Aaron, my narcissistic lover, came into my life in the summer of 2005. When we met, I was going through a lot, so admittedly I had my rose-tinted spectacles firmly on and transmitting at full beam. I saw only the good in him, which clouded my better judgement of this apparently loving and selfless man. Over the next five years, Aaron derailed me from my plans and life purpose, or so I thought at the time. Now, I believe it was all set out within a divine plan, to teach me and shape me into the woman I became. Everything happens for a reason.

Aaron was certainly charming. A businessman, he wore tailored suits and polished his shoes daily. He was tall, with an athletic stature, dark hair, piercing blue eyes and an enticing smile. He was in his mid-thirties, while I was twenty-six. I'd never been drawn to older men before, so this was a novelty for me. It all started out like a fairy tale, which I guess I was craving at the time. Although I couldn't see it, I was at my most vulnerable emotionally.

So, where to begin? Perhaps with how our life paths crossed. I'd just returned from Australia to spend the summer preparing for my friend's wedding, and to spend time in the UK with loved ones. I felt I was at a crossroads in my life. I'd always been a free spirit, but I didn't know whether to return to Australia at the end of my break.

Upon arriving in the UK, I went to stay with friends in a small village. This village is like no other place I have visited to date – and given that I grew up in the rough East End of London, this is saying a lot. It's a picturesque place on the outskirts of the Cotswolds, with several pubs and a small shop, but if it sounds pleasant, I can assure you it's not. As I soon came to learn, the biggest gossips and troublemakers resided here. My good friend Kelly, whose wedding it was, would often say that it was a village full of housewives with nothing better to do than to look down their noses at you, and to call out the 'specks' in other people's eyes, without ever examining their own flaws and imperfections. What an idyllic yet toxic place to live this would become. Now, don't get me wrong, not everyone living in the village was like this, otherwise I wouldn't have been staying there. Kelly is kind and humble in nature. But some of the mothers, whose children attended the local faith school with my goddaughters, were not always the most caring of souls. My mother's old saying of, "Pay everyone you meet with kind, and it will serve you well," obviously wasn't popular here. This was also where Aaron resided.

I spent the summer dividing my time between helping Kelly get ready for the wedding and visiting my father Daniel and older brother Johnny in East London. It was lovely to spend so much time with the people who mattered to me most.

Meeting Aaron was both unexpected and untimely. It was a Friday night, and I'd planned to head into London to spend the weekend with my dad. I can still remember my excitement at driving Zara, my Mini Cooper S, all the way into the city. However, when I went to start the engine, her battery was flat. I was rather upset by this but wise enough to know it was out of my control, as by now all the local garages had shut. I resigned myself to the fact that nothing could be done until the morning. Instead, Friday night would be spent in with Kelly and her family. However, the cheeky little minx had other plans for me. She wanted me to attend a football club event with her and her hubby Joe at the local pub. There was going to be a tribute band playing and, knowing that Joe would go off with his footy mates, she didn't want to be left on her own.

Kelly pleaded with me to accompany her and reassured me that we would have fun. How could I say no? After all, she was one of my best mates and, with or without alcohol, we always managed to have a good time together. So, putting my disappointed feelings aside, I changed out of the onesie I'd been wearing and off we went to the pub. Once inside, I spotted many friendly, familiar faces – people I hadn't seen in a long time. It was lovely to be greeted with such warmth, and once I'd caught up with everyone, Kelly and I made a beeline for the bar. As she had anticipated, Joe had got chatting to the lads with whom he played weekly football.

Whilst queuing to get a drink, I noticed a tall, dark-haired man with the most soul piercing blue eyes at the opposite end of the bar. It was late evening and I distinctly remember how odd it seemed for him to be fully suited and booted, with a pair of shades nicely balanced on his forehead. I could not help but stare in wonder. Why was he dressed so smartly so late on a Friday night? Had he just come from a work meeting? As I stared at him, he waved at me, as if he knew me. Instinctively, I waved back. After all, he did seem familiar.

Kelly noticed and grabbed my hand. "What are you doing? He's married. Don't wave at him."

"But I know him, we've met before."

Kelly explained that this couldn't be the case, as he

was relatively new to the village. I was shocked, as it really did feel like we had crossed paths before. I was trying to connect the dots. Sometime later, Aaron made his way over to Kelly and me.

"Hello, Lovina, how are you?"

"See, Kelly, I told you I knew him," I burst out rather unexpectedly.

Aaron just looked at me and smiled incessantly like a Cheshire cat. I noticed the perfectly balanced shades were Louis Vuitton. He asked me if I would like a drink, but I declined graciously and followed Kelly to a table. As the night progressed, I noticed my friend becoming more and more tipsy. She was due to babysit her niece the next morning, so I reminded her to slow down. She replied, "Lovina and Aaron sitting in a tree, K-I-S-S-I-N-G."

This is when I knew she had consumed way too many G&Ts.

"Kelly," I said, "you know I've had a rocky time since things ended with Andre."

Andre was my ex, whom I'd split up from six months ago.

Kelly looked at me with that fuzzy, vacant expression that tipsy people tend to have.

"I need time to find myself again. You of all people know how it hurts to part ways with someone, and for the next year, self-care, love and healing are my priority."

My mind drifted as I reminisced about Andre. We had met in 2001, in my special place, my spiritual home of Bali, Indonesia. It was a beautiful November day, with a thirty-degree heat and no wind. For the time of year, this was rather unusual, as it was the rainy season . . .

"Jesus, Jesus, it's a Jesus moment, I can feel it."

Kelly was shouting out at me, bringing me back to the present moment.

"OK," I said. "Aaron is at the bar with his back to me, talking to some people. If he turns around to look at me, within my countdown of ten, I will call him over to chat."

Anyhow, as sure as the ocean is made up of water, I'd only made it to seven when Aaron chose to turn around and wave at me.

"See, it is as if by Jesus!" shouted Kelly. 'So, Starr, you have to call him over and talk to him, right now!

"I thought you said he was married," I replied sternly. "I don't do married men, my love. I am a good woman."

Kelly replied, "Since Aaron has been staring at you all night, I asked Joe, and he said he is going through a divorce."

So, I waved back, and Aaron came over. We sat and talked for hours, or so it seemed. I listened to him attentively. I could see his soul, and with it feel the pain of his many years spent in an unhappy marriage. The mood went from a happy and explorative one, as we learned about who we were as people and talked about our respective lives, to one that was sombre and sad. Aaron continued to speak at length about a controlling home environment. He explained that he wasn't allowed to see his children, even though he lived in the same house as them. He opened up about his wife's control and her inability to empathise or be compassionate towards him. All I wanted to do was give this man the world's biggest hug. It was pretty distressing to feel the pain and suffering that radiated from him. Even now, as I type these words, I can remember his deep sorrow. Aaron spoke highly of his children, but his interactions with them were constantly being controlled by his wife. He was clearly not coping with his domestic life. I instantly felt the need to pray for him. So, I did, even though we were in the middle of a lively pub, filled with people elated and drunk on happy vibes.

I placed my hand on his shoulder, as I simultaneously began to speak out. "Lord Jesus, I am a daughter of a King of Kings, and I ask that you hear my prayer. You are Christ, who is able to make the impossible possible. I hold before you Aaron, at the foot of the cross. I ask you, Prince of Peace, to place your hands upon his shoulders. Please comfort and reassure him that you are always there, carrying him when it all gets too much. I pray that his wife's heart is softened, and that she allows Aaron time with his cherubs. That you would help her, Lord Jesus, to reconcile her differences with this man before me, for the sake of the children's wellbeing."

This was a defining moment in terms of what was to come next. As the night drew to a close, we all said our goodbyes and I left the pub with Kelly and Joe.

2

FAITH IS BELIEVING THAT WHICH
YOU DO NOT SEE

Sidestepping my lover-to-be for a moment, I thought it best to explain my faith, especially as you have just read that I prayed out loud for Aaron the first time we met. Also, my faith was one of the strongholds that helped me to survive the narcissist in my life.

My childhood home was free from religion and other people's expectations regarding what I was to believe. My mother, Sandra, and father, Daniel, were both of the opinion that faith comes from within. This meant that neither of them ever talked about God. When I was eight, I can remember being drawn to the sound of Sunday School music being played at the church next to our house. Every Sunday, late morning, I would hear the same songs, which compelled me to investigate further. On one such Sunday, I took myself off to the church, which I continued to attend for a few years. Mum and Dad neither encouraged nor deterred me from going. It was always my choice. They were proud of me for exploring my belief system at such a young age. Then, when my mother passed away to ovarian cancer when I was just eighteen, I lost my way on my spiritual journey.

During my university years studying for a degree in medicine, I began to question life. I was involved in a serious car accident that should have resulted in my death. However, I walked away from the wreckage of my car unscathed and in awe of how I had survived such a major accident. This led me on a journey of faith, to discover what was protecting, guiding and helping me on my life's path.

The awakening of the truth within and the strengthening of my faith was to come a few years later, when I was mentally unwell. In fact, I was so poorly and in darkness that I would constantly question my own faculties. The huge change in my demeanour and personality was clear for my loved ones to see. I had lost weight, and the light in my eyes and my physical capabilities had diminished. When I was really bad, I can remember turning up at my friend Brie's house and asking, "How do I shower?"

I was guided to sell my flat, go to Australia, where my boyfriend Andre lived, and attend church. For those of you reading this who have no faith, I can understand how this might appear quite bizarre. At certain times of my life, it would have done to me, too. But at an inherent soul level, something inside me knew that this was the move I needed to make in order to heal and restore my true self. What a leap of faith! To sell my home and leave all that I knew back in the UK to go and live with my boyfriend Down Under. And all on a tourist visa! But I trusted and believed that this move would save me. Utter craziness, right? But I still did it.

Using what little energy I could muster, I sorted out the sale of my flat, which would fund my journey. By this point, I'd been suffering from insomnia for over ten months, which would be enough to drive anyone insane, but I knew deep down that I wasn't crazy. Unwell as I was, I could tell this was the right thing to do. I'm sure those of you reading this with faith will be able to relate wholeheartedly to my story.

Now, while I am a woman of faith, I am not religious. Faith is believing 'that which you do not see'. Jesus had faith in everyone, and He walked this Earth as a healing man. Jesus was to be the turning point in restoring my mental state and balance, and as a result, I have so much conviction in the unseen.

In Australia, the church I attended with Andre arranged a women-only weekend. This is known by those of faith worldwide as the Colour Conference. It was here that my mental state was restored and my gift for helping others became clear. Jesus healed me and showed me 'the more' that from a young age I'd known existed. Again, I am not religious, and I don't preach to others, but my faith is at the heart of who I am and in everything that I do to help humanity, both now and until I draw my last breath.

3

IT'S THE SMALL THINGS THAT COUNT

AARON CONTACTED ME TWO WEEKS AFTER OUR PATHS had crossed. I was driving to church and my phone began to beep. Something within me made me pull over to check it. Aaron had texted to ask if I was free to meet at the local for a drink and a chat about his children. I remember thinking to myself that it was way too early in the day for anything alcoholic, and I hoped he just meant coffee. Nevertheless, I agreed to meet with him. After sending my reply, I felt a flow of energy run through my body, as if the Holy Spirit was present. I knew this feeling was a sign for me to act and be of service to a man in distress and pain, even if that meant changing my plans and missing church.

When I arrived at the pub, I couldn't see Aaron anywhere. He had strategically placed himself by a window around the corner, close to the pool table. I didn't frequent the pub, so I had no idea that this spot was a prime place for those who didn't want to be seen by people passing on the main road. Luckily, Aaron noticed my arrival and called me over to his nook. He was reading *The Telegraph* while drinking a beer. I did not think to ask, "Why a drink so early?" Maybe if I had then none of this story would have come to be. Maybe I would have seen sooner that he was addicted to alcohol. Instead, I seemed to be completely smitten by this individual, who the Holy Spirit had placed in my heart. I sat with Aaron, coffee in hand, and listened attentively to his story. He poured out so much pain and hurt, and I was completely transfixed. As I'm such a sensitive soul, it had been easy for Aaron to reel me in. Little did I know that I was about to become a modern-day Florence Nightingale to the man before me. I remember time passing quickly, as Aaron spoke of his miserable marriage and his controlling wife's poor mental health. He was devastated that he barely had contact with his two children, despite the fact they all lived in the same house.

Aaron came across as intelligent, kind and caring. Why would I doubt him? But for a split second or so, I did, and then it passed. I chose to ignore my gut feeling. After all, my mum had taught me from a young age that there are always two sides to a story.

As the day went on, we were both feeling hungry and Aaron suggested a roast dinner, which involved going to a different pub. We ended up spending from the late morning to the late evening together. I enjoyed the spontaneity of the day and didn't want it to end. I felt connected to Aaron, as if I had known him much longer. As the night drew in, he dropped me back to where my car was parked in the village and returned to his family home.

During that summer, I can remember one defining moment that hooked me into Aaron. I had taken a friend's son for lunch and we bumped into him in the high street. As usual, he was all suited and booted. I invited him to have lunch with us, and he accepted. Afterwards, we all walked back to where my mini, Zara, was parked and went our separate ways. No less than an hour later, Aaron called me to ask where I was. I replied that I was at Kelly's house. Within ten minutes, he was knocking at the door.

"Close your eyes and hold out your hands," he said when I opened the door. I felt rather nervous, as I had only known him for a few weeks. As I did what he had instructed, I felt my tummy doing flips. I then felt a strangely shaped object being placed in my hands. I hadn't a clue what it was. When I opened my eyes, I saw that it was a lightbulb. I looked up at Aaron, who beamed at me before explaining that he had seen me drive off in Zara and had noticed that my brake light wasn't working. He had gone to purchase a replacement bulb and then come over to fit it. His random act of kindness resonated with me, and I was overwhelmed. I remember watching Aaron fix my brake light and thinking to myself, *He is meant to be working but has gone out of his way to help me*. These small things speak volumes to me. It was at this point that I dropped my guard with Aaron. He'd got me hook, line and sinker.

After changing my brake light, Aaron left, telling me that he would return after his children had been put to bed. He explained that once his kids had gone to sleep, his wife would goad him, hurling abuse at him until he locked himself in the conservatory, fearing for his own safety. I felt so saddened by this and invited him to come over each evening to escape the hell that he had so emotively described. I didn't know it at the time, but the conservatory was actually where he went to drink more wine after getting back from the pub, and that on some nights he never even made it back to the family home.

In the bliss of my ignorance, the weeks that followed were filled with many happy and memorable moments, as I enjoyed the rest of the summer months with friends and Aaron. I guess by this point we were officially dating. As the season drew to a close, we met up to celebrate Kelly's birthday at the local pub. Halfway through the meal, I noticed Aaron on his iPad. Next minute, he turned to me and said, "How do you fancy going to Rome with me for a few days?"

Being the free-spirited soul that I am, I immediately replied, "Yeah, sure."

Aaron went silent again. A few more minutes passed before he announced, "It's booked, we leave Monday."

I felt a mixture of excitement and fear. Aaron had just been spontaneous and thoughtful, which I decided were good qualities for a partner to possess. But he had a family at home and was currently going through a divorce. How could he just up and go? Unfortunately, I was so swept away by this whirlwind romance and constant love bombing that I wasn't thinking straight. You see, I believe that marriage is precious, and that when you choose to commit to someone else it really should be for life. Technically, Aaron was still tied to someone else. Despite my reservations, I ignored that niggling voice in my head, allowing my more adventurous, naughty one to convince me to go to Rome 'as friends'. I told myself that this would make it OK. After all, this man was in desperate need of a confidant, someone to help him see the positive in life, and who was I not to help him, especially when I knew this was my calling in life?

In accepting Aaron's romantic invitation, I chose to ignore my inner guide and turn a blind eye to the baggage he was carrying and the sort of person he really was. It's my aim to help you avoid making the same mistakes.

LEARNING POINTS: HOW TO RECOGNISE A NARCISSIST

- There is always a hooking point for the narcissist. Following Aaron's random act of kindness, I let him into my circle of trust. He had already identified how much the small things count for me, and how they impact my being. I used to think these acts revealed a person's true heart, but I've since realised that a narcissist will use them for their own gain.

- The narcissist will study you to find out how they can tap into you. When it came to my relationship with Aaron, my trait of only seeing the good in others and defending the weak led to my demise emotionally.

- At first, narcissists are exceptionally charming and will tend to dominate the conversation by talking about how great they are. Blindsided by their charisma, you might not even notice this.

- You will find yourself doing way too much physically, emotionally and mentally to keep the narcissist afloat, especially if addictions to drink or drugs are present. Become aware of how much you do in comparison to them. There will usually be an imbalance, in their favour rather than in yours.

- Narcissists will tend to focus solely on you, as they won't have many, if any, long-term friends. You may notice that they only have casual mates and buddies, whom they will often trash when they talk about them. In time, they will lash out at you when you want to hang out with your own friends. You will be accused of not spending enough time with them and will be made to feel guilty. In some scenarios, the narcissist will berate you for the type of friends you keep.

4

LOVE BOMBED

From the moment Aaron booked for us to go to Rome, all I could think about was how romantic he was. I kept wondering, *Is this the man for me?* He seemed to be everything I'd ever wanted.

The love bombing started on the flight over to Rome, when he cuddled into me. "Sweetie," he whispered. "You truly are one in a million and I'm so blessed that you've come into my life. You really are an angel, and I cannot thank you enough for all the help you've given me."

"It's nothing. I want to help you to heal yourself," I replied.

He kept handing me the duty-free catalogue. Every time I put it aside, he put it back in my hand. "Have a look for something nice," he said. "I want to get you something to remind you of our first trip together."

I eventually gave in and flicked through it. I'm not one for gifts, nor are my affections easily won over by material things, but Aaron seemed genuine in his wish to buy me something, and he was incredibly charming with it. Just to stop his incessant pestering, I chose some Ralph Lauren *Romance* perfume. It's been a firm favourite of mine since I was eighteen and a basic go to for a floral aroma that is not too overpowering.

Aaron had booked us a hotel on the outskirts of the city centre, so we could commute in for the restaurants and sights and travel back to our sanctuary whenever we felt like it. As Aaron was working remotely, we spent our first day by the hotel pool. He'd failed to tell me before we left that he would still need to take calls twenty-four seven. His job as an insurance broker was clearly demanding. But even so, why hadn't he taken the time off? I wondered if he'd told his wife that he was going away on a business trip. I pushed my reservations to one side. I was still in fairy tale mode and wasn't too concerned with his past or how he may be treating the mother of his children. He was showering me with constant affection and complimenting both my mind and physical appearance. I felt incredibly special. All loved up, I continued to ignore any warning signs, as I lost myself to the endless kisses, cuddles and sweet utterances. Feeling high on life and love, I could see a definite future with Aaron. Come what may, I felt we connected on a level that was worth the time, investment and commitment of self.

Whenever we ate out, Aaron would drink endless amounts of wine – carafe after carafe. I remember commenting on his love for red wine and how much he consumed compared to what I could handle. By the end of the night, Aaron would already have drunk the equivalent of over two – nearly three – bottles. On the second day, he even started drinking at midday. In the evening, we went for a meal, with yet more vino, and when we arrived back at the hotel at around eleven o'clock, he ordered a bottle of Chateauneuf-du-Pape from reception, to have on our room's balcony. An hour in and things started turning ugly. He started to bellow at me, for no apparent reason and with nothing triggering it.

"I am not good for you, Lovina, you need to leave when you can."

When I went to give him a cuddle, he pushed me away. "Aren't you listening? I'm no good for you!"

I was pretty shocked by his behaviour. Even so, I went to grab him again, this time holding him tightly.

"Sweetie, get off me, you deserve better. I come with baggage, and lots of it!"

"I don't see your children as baggage," I replied. "I see them as beautiful beings that are part of you."

Aaron released himself from my tight grip and walked off the balcony to go to bed.

I followed. "Why are you no good for me, handsome? Why would you say such a thing?"

Aaron shut down and refused to talk to me. Both bemused and frustrated, I listened to the voice of reason and decided not to further agitate this already emotional man. The next day, the last one of our mini break, we'd planned to visit the Vatican, and Aaron woke up being his usual affectionate and loving self, as if the night before had never happened. He didn't apologise for or explain his outburst, and I chose to let it go and concentrate instead on our day of adventure. After all, I don't believe in living in the past and always try to focus on the present.

LEARNING POINTS: BE KIND TO YOURSELF WHEN YOU FALL FOR THE CHARM

- For narcissists, love bombing is a manipulative tactic, which they use to reel in their target. You may not be aware of it, as they will play the part of everything you have ever wanted in a partner. They have a tendency to shower their lover with both excessive affection and gifts, which is done simply to gain control. But how can you tell if this is different to the usual honeymoon phase that most people in a new relationship experience? Well, expect them to turn on you further down the line.

- If you do fall into a narcissist's trap, be kind to yourself. After all, it's what they're good at. I was a successful lady in her twenties and still fell victim to one. It can happen to people of any age and background. Be sure not to beat yourself up over it.

5

OUT OF SIGHT, OUT OF MIND

In the autumn of 2005, I was forced to reflect on my original plan to return to Australia. Seeing and sensing that my dad was unwell was one part to it, and then unexpectedly meeting Aaron added to my conundrum.

Meanwhile, Aaron had to go to Asia for work and decided to have a holiday Down Under with me first. I figured it would be a good opportunity to get to know him better. On the day of our departure, as we boarded our Singapore Airlines flight to Sydney, he took a call from his ex-wife, Anne. She started shouting down the phone at him, stating she knew he was with me and that we were going away together. Aaron argued back before ending the call. The flight was long, and we spent the time eating, sleeping and watching the inflight entertainment. Upon our arrival in Sydney, we took a flight over to Perth to stay with my cousins, who had been living in Australia for the past twenty years. During our stay, I noticed Aaron drinking more and more, but he seemed to be getting on well with my relatives, so I chose to let the four bottles of wine a night slide. Looking back, I know this was a clear warning sign that he had a serious addiction, but at the time I brushed it aside. During the first few days of our time together, Aaron's ex-wife called to say that she had left the marital home and taken the children with her. Aaron was completely shell shocked and devastated. He consumed even more alcohol to numb the pain. I tried to console him and cuddle him to sleep, but he seemed to have shut down emotionally. The following morning, he turned to me in bed and shouted, "You are not helping, what have you done to help me?!?"

Without waiting for a reply, he continued to bellow at me, repeating, "What have you done to help me?"

As he was shouting, he wagged his index finger at me incessantly. "You are stupid, so fucking stupid! You are just like her."

I was completely stunned and lost for words. I didn't have time to feel or react – I simply hadn't expected to be woken up and have abuse hurled at me. What had happened to a pleasant cuddle and a, "Morning, lovely"?

The Florence Nightingale in me put it down to the trauma of the night before, and like his drinking, I chose to let it go. After all, Aaron had just been told that he would be returning to an empty home. I have always tried to put myself in others' shoes and identify their coping mechanisms. This meant that once again, I accepted Aaron's unacceptable abuse. I told myself that his irrational behaviour was down to the pain he was suffering and, therefore, it was forgivable.

After our holiday, I flew to Bali. When Aaron returned to the UK, I heard through the grapevine that he kept a low profile. He wasn't seen in the pubs or at the shops. Worried about him, as soon as I got home, I visited him at his sprawling, detached six-bedder surrounded by acres of land. It was a picturesque property but far too big for someone to be living in alone.

As I drove up the driveway, I can distinctly remember noticing that all the lights were off. I parked near the main entrance and spent at least five minutes banging loudly on the front door. I was about to leave when Aaron came to open it. Standing before me was a shell of the man I'd met back in the summer. He seemingly hadn't changed his clothes or shaved for weeks. He resembled a train wreck. The sharp suit had been replaced with loungewear, and he was crying and clearly intoxicated. Wishing to console this truly broken man, I asked to come in. It was clear to see how lost and alone he had become living in this huge house by himself. As I walked in, I noticed all the furniture and soft furnishings had been removed, making the house feel even bigger. It felt as cold as a morgue, and all I can remember thinking was how lucky I was to have been brought up in a loving home. We didn't have the money Aaron and his family had once enjoyed together, but our place was filled with the one thing money can't buy. It's love that makes a house a home, not the expensive things it contains.

When I choose to love someone, I love unconditionally. The man before me clearly needed to be loved, so it happened quite naturally. I let down my guard and was drawn into wanting to heal his broken heart and soul. I could feel all the pain oozing out of him whilst he stood at the door lost and very much alone. The intensity of it switched my innate healing side into hyperdrive. I longed to find ways to show him the abundance of unconditional love in his life, and that he was worthy of it. But, as I would come to learn over the course of nearly five years in a dysfunctional relationship, trying to help a lost soul who isn't willing to help himself is a whole different ball game. I poured my heart, soul, love and time into this man and his children only to ultimately leave with nothing: no love, kindness, respect or loyalty.

As you continue to read about this journey of mine, you will come to learn the many signs and traits of a narcissist. I can remember being allowed into the house and making us both a cup of tea, while listening to him and trying to console him. However, at the time, I failed to realise that this was a man who loved to tell a story; a white lie or two, if you will – the kind my mother would be turning in her grave over. To think that I, her daughter, played a part in his stories and lies disappoints me to this day. Unfortunately, this was the case in the first eighteen months of our relationship together, as I had no idea who or what I was dealing with. His manipulation skills were of a gold-star standard.

Aaron was like a broken record when it came to how badly his wife had treated him at home and how unsafe he felt. Being a natural defender of the weak, this resonated with me. I simply wished to help this person, whom I was also becoming extremely fond of. What I didn't know at the time was that he rarely told me the truth. For instance, back when his wife and kids still lived at home, I didn't know that he often rocked up drunk in the early hours and caused a scene, waking up the entire family. His behaviour came to light via emails from his ex-wife's solicitor. Apparently, he'd been doing it for nearly a year before we met in the summer of 2005.

Since our parting of ways, I have come to learn of the other women from the local pub whom Aaron had, shall we say, 'befriended' before our paths crossed. Apparently, he would take them back to his other property in a nearby village, before returning to his marital home when he'd finished 'entertaining' them. This would explain why his ex-wife disliked me so much. She thought I was the reason why Aaron returned home at four in the morning and disturbed her and her cherubs' sleep. But this atrocious behaviour and poor conduct had been going on for months before I came into the picture. By that time, Anne had already initiated the divorce.

LEARNING POINTS: TRAITS OF A NARCISSIST

- A narcissist is good at deception and is often secretive. These are the two main traits to look out for if you suspect your partner or someone you know might be one. There are always two sides to a story, but I chose to believe Aaron's version of events because I was emotionally involved with him. We all like to think we can trust our partners, right? I guess I was hoping that he was someone I could have faith in. After all, he was a professional man, an upstanding member of the community and a father of two. But when it comes to a narcissist, nothing is ever quite what it seems.
- A narcissist will constantly pick on you. At first, when Aaron started doing this to me, I figured he was just teasing me, but it soon became constant verbal abuse. Everything you do, from what you eat and wear to the

people you hang out with can be a problem for the narcissist. They may also call you names and make jokes that are not funny in an attempt to lower your self-esteem and increase their own. This makes them feel powerful.

- A narcissist will love getting a reaction from you, but responding to the negative things they say will only reinforce their behaviour, because it shows them they have the power to affect another person's emotional state.

6

AND SO THE EMOTIONAL CONTROL BEGINS

IT WAS IN DECEMBER THAT I MET AARON'S CHILDREN, Charlie, 13, and Arabella, 10. At the time, I had no idea that Arabella and I would go on to form a long-term bond, both emotionally and spiritually. I can remember our meeting as if it were yesterday. She was this beautiful little cherub who was so full of energy. It was clear that she was extremely charismatic but at the same time a little on the shy side.

This was the first weekend that Aaron was able to see his children since Anne had moved them out of the family home. I felt a little uneasy being invited to meet them so early on, but Aaron pleaded with me to come and support him. He felt he wouldn't be able to cope on his own. "Sweetie, it would mean a lot to me if you could help me," he said.

Of course, that pulled on my heartstrings and I

agreed without hesitation. I didn't even consider how my actions might affect Anne's emotional state.

We spent most of our time together playing board games. Then, as the day came to a close, Aaron asked the children if they would like "Daddy's friend" to stay over. I remember feeling pretty shocked by this, as it smacked of manipulation, and I just wanted to go home. I believe this was the second defining moment of this narcissist getting his claws into me. Even though we were only a few months into dating, Aaron was creating an emotional bridge between his children and me. Narcissists need to exert emotional control in their relationships, and so he was forging these family ties, which would make it harder for me to leave in the long-term. Aaron knew that I longed to be a mother, and he capitalised on this knowledge. The children liked me, so he must have figured that I could take over nurturing them. This kind of thing spells happy days for a narcissist, as they hate having to be selfless. At this point, I was a high-ranking commodity for Aaron, as I would be until I stopped serving a purpose. The time will come when you can no longer give the narcissist what they need, and they will stop walking on burning coals for you. He or she will either bully you into leaving or discard you with no consideration of your emotional needs. They may have affairs to fulfil their addictive personality, all while pushing you aside both physically and emotionally.

~

Christmas 2005 brought quality time with Aaron, Arabella and Charlie. I arranged to take them all to Winter Wonderland in Hyde Park. I thought it would inject some much-needed fun into the time that the children spent with their father. I loved getting to know their family dynamics. When he was in a good mood, Charlie was a delight to be around. He despised injustice, especially when his dad blamed him for something he hadn't done. The day was magical from start to end, and I especially enjoyed seeing the joy that Aaron's children gave him. His face lit up whenever he saw that they were enjoying themselves. But he became anxious whenever we were in crowds, worried that he might lose sight of either or both of them. He was especially protective of Arabella, and I had to constantly reassure him that she and her brother were safe. Despite this, we made some life-long memories, from seeing ice sculptures, to riding the ghost train and watching a live acrobatic show in the big tent. Seeing Aaron openly express his love for his son and daughter gave me the hope that we would eventually have a child of our own. Little did I know that over time my wish to become a mum would be used as leverage against me. It would be the dangling carrot in our relationship, which would keep me there for the next four years.

We saw Aaron's children again for the second week of the Christmas holidays. Aaron insisted that I be with them for the duration. Given that I had only just met the children, I felt extremely uncomfortable about this, but at the same time, given his anxieties, I didn't want to leave Aaron hosting them on his own. Outside of work, he was barely coping with the demands of his life. His job took a lot out of him. He was regularly on the phone for hours at a time. I guess he had to be to earn the kind of salary he was on. The company he worked for seemed intent on drawing blood from a stone. Taking all this into account, I agreed to go over and help him. I have a fun disposition and my silly nature means that kids naturally gravitate towards me. Again, at the end of our first day together, Aaron asked Arabella and Charlie if they wanted "Daddy's friend" to stay the night.

I immediately pulled him to one side. "I'll go home and come back in the morning to see you all," I said.

I didn't realise how much alcohol Aaron had already consumed. I thought he'd only had a few small beers, but close up, his eyes told a different story. They were glassy and red, and throughout the rest of the evening, he was full-on silly. He was being oversensitive and got upset when he decided to dance and none of us would get up and join him. Worried about leaving him to cope with the kids on his own, I agreed to stay, on the condition I slept in the spare room. This was not to Aaron's liking, but I felt it was the right thing to do with regards to the children and my faith.

The following day, Aaron asked me if I would like to join them to see in the New Year. I felt drawn to being around them and readily agreed. Little did I know that the start of 2006 would be very different to the romantic vision I'd conjured in my head.

Picture it, as I set the scene. We had indulged in some party food and, like thousands of others around the country, retreated to the living room to watch *Jools' Annual Hootenanny* on the TV. Aaron was up dancing with Arabella, and we were all laughing and joking. I play fought with Charlie while Aaron brought some more food and drink from the kitchen. It seemed to be the perfect evening. Alas, as the night wore on, the glassy-eyed version of Aaron joined the party. As we counted down to the New Year, he had us all stand up and interlock our hands, to do Hogmanay the "right" way. As we tried to shake hands together in this intwined state, Aaron started to get frustrated with us. Charlie and I both dropped a link, which outraged him. When we failed to interlock our arms again, Aaron shouted at his son, "Why can't you get a simple thing right?"

As Charlie turned to his dad, Aaron continued the tirade. "Do you know how fucking disrespectful you are being by purposely letting go of our hands?"

Charlie, barely thirteen, looked flabbergasted by his father's behaviour towards him. I instantly took Aaron aside to try and calm him down, but he wouldn't let the issue drop. By this point, Arabella said she wanted to go to her room. Now Aaron turned on her. "You don't want to spend any time with your dad," he hissed. "Only your mother. You always choose her!"

He went on to accuse Arabella of treating him badly. Disliking what I was seeing, I chose to intervene. This is when I got the first inkling of what I had taken on in this relationship. Aaron proceeded to turn on me, pinning me against the wall and ranting and raving like a madman. "All you do, Anne, is take, take, take. You're always spending other people's money."

I was so totally taken aback by Aaron calling me by his ex's name that I just took the abuse. Also, I didn't want to cause more of a scene for the children, so I absorbed all of his emotional hurt and went to bed. Aaron chose to remain downstairs, with the TV blaring until the early hours. When I went to get a glass of water at daybreak, I found him asleep on the sofa. He looked incredibly uncomfortable, so I decided to wake him and tell him to go to his own bed.

When the morning came, I got up early, as usual, and decided to tidy up the lounge and kitchen. "Happy New Year to me," I said out loud to myself, as I reflected on the night before. Aaron came down soon after and I told him that I had to leave. I explained how abusive he had been to me and that it was not right. He begged me to stay and explained that this was the first real chunk of time he'd had with his children in ages. The drink and the memories of his ex-wife had got to him. He begged me for forgiveness and for me not to end what we had. I explained that he kept calling me by his ex's name, and that he'd been both physically and verbally aggressive. Aaron looked horrified. Clearly, he'd been in blackout mode at the time and couldn't remember a thing. He apologised sincerely.

I know that some of you reading this may be thinking that I should have left there and then, and for good. I totally get that, and if the same situation arose again, I would do just that. But at that point in time, I chose to give Aaron the benefit of the doubt. I wanted to continue my support of him and his children.

LEARNING POINTS: THE 'RED FLAGS' AND INTUITIVE FEELINGS

- Wake up to those early warning signs and your gut feelings. They are usually right, and yet we can all ignore them. By pushing them aside, you may become powerless to a one-sided love affair. Seeing signs and recognising the lack of empathy within the other person will help you to protect your own sense of self.

- A narcissist can be childlike, so watch out for this type of behaviour. I was dating a man who did not love himself. When things didn't go his way, he threw his toys out of the pram and screamed the house down.
- Be mindful of being blindsided by your own good nature. I only allowed myself to see the good in the narcissist in my life, even when he shouted in my face. This trait will keep the narcissist's true nature off your radar.
- A need within you to heal will camouflage signs of the emotional selfishness that a narcissist usually displays. Take note of what you tell yourself to excuse their bad behaviour.
- A narcissist is someone who only thinks of their own needs, unless behaving otherwise benefits them in some way. Think about whether they have ever put you first.
- They will not consider how their actions (and inaction) will affect the emotional and mental wellbeing of those around them.
- I believe a narcissist is incapable of loving another without professional intervention. They will only appear to love you because there is something in it for them.

- Narcissists need to exert emotional control in their relationships, which can make it harder for their partner to leave in the long-term.

7

BETRAYAL AND DENIAL

BEING SUCH A PERSONABLE BEING, I TEND TO MAKE new friends wherever I go. I get this from my dad. He could light up a room and would talk to anyone. It was through chatting to a lady from my gym that I was invited to a Valentine's comedy event. By this point, Aaron and I had been together for eight months, and he referred to me as his partner, so I thought it would be nice for us to do something special on our first February 14th together. It was a night I will never forget, but for all the wrong reasons.

Upon our arrival at the hotel, where the event was being held, we were seated with some other people on a circular table, only a few of whom I knew. The lady next to me seemed to be on her own, so I immediately introduced myself, knowing how I would feel if I was the only one at the table without a partner. She was called Julie, and in the run-up to our three-course meal being served, we chatted about our lives and all manner of things. We realised we had a friend in common and the conversation flowed. I love socialising and meeting new people, and before long, Julie was opening up to me about her hardships and losses. I felt that she and Aaron had a lot in common, having both been through so much with ex partners. I decided they might find it healing to have a chat with one another. Looking back, and knowing what I know now, I can see how naive and foolish I was being.

As the night progressed, Aaron got progressively more intoxicated and over friendly with the others, especially Julie. I completely trusted him, so I left them in deep conversation about their past lives. After we'd eaten, I went to the bar to have a chat with some people I knew and get some more wine. To this day, I still can't remember about three hours of my life after this point. I'd only had two glasses of wine, which wasn't enough to black out by any means, so why this happened is a complete mystery.

What I can recall is going on a hunt for Aaron after finding him missing from the table. Eventually, I stumbled outside and into the grounds of the venue. What happened next pains me to type and share, as when I give my heart, I give it fully, which at that moment, I really wish wasn't the case. In the car park adjoining the hotel, I saw Aaron and Julie standing by a car. The door was open, and they were leaning in for a kiss. As I watched their lips touch, the pain I felt was so gut wrenching I almost threw up. Why would the man I'd supported through his divorce, enabling him to keep his job and cope with his children coming to visit, do such a thing to me? Did I deserve this kind of treatment? All I can remember is shouting at them, before falling to the ground. To onlookers, I must have appeared a drunken mess, as there were floods of tears rolling down my cheeks and my eyes were smudged with mascara. I watched as Aaron ushered Julie into the car, which I realised was a taxi. She left immediately and he walked over to help me up. I am not proud of my actions, but I pushed him off me and told him to leave me alone. He had cheated on me right under my nose and then had the bare-faced cheek to tell me to stay calm, so he wouldn't lose face in front of onlookers.

Now, I can't remember much more after that, except that I must have taken myself to the steps up to the hotel, as I found myself sitting on them and shouting all manner of things at my 'Valentine'. The staff came out and advised me to go home. Unfortunately, all the taxis were taken so I had to walk with Aaron to his house, which was two villages away. Walking all those miles in high heels sucked and was probably just as painful as seeing my man kissing another woman. I can remember cursing Aaron and asking him to stay away from me. The whole night was so odd. I'd 'lost' time between going to the bar and seeing Aaron and Julie kissing, and I only have hazy memories of the walk back. It felt the same as when someone slipped a date rape drug into my drink when I was on holiday in New Zealand. Luckily, nothing bad had happened to me back then, but the memory loss was disconcerting.

When I woke up the next morning, Aaron wasn't beside me. I texted the friend Julie and I shared to ask for her number, so I could confront her about what had happened. Julie informed me that Aaron had already been on the phone to her and had asked to go round and see her, so he could apologise in person. She told me it was him I needed to speak to, but repeatedly said that it was just a drunken kiss, a mistake. She reassured me that Aaron really loved me and felt awful over messing up due to being under the influence. To be fair on Julie, she was both sincere and extremely apologetic. At the time, it never even crossed my mind that I wasn't the first one Aaron had reached out to. And nor did I wonder why he had Julie's number when it was just a drunken snog. On reflection, a decade on, I feel it was very much planned. He must have given her his number, and vice versa, before she got into the taxi. Who in a loving, trusting relationship does that?

Instead of walking out there and then, I allowed Aaron to explain himself. He was sincere and begged me not to abandon what we had, insisting with passion and conviction that we made a great couple and that he had been incredibly stupid to put our relationship in jeopardy.

Seeing me wavering, Aaron turned the conversation around. He told me I had "lost the plot" during the walk home and that when we'd arrived back at his, I'd ripped the shirt off his back in a fit of rage. I thought it was justified considering what I'd witnessed, but then Aaron claimed that I'd also hit him. Despite knowing that I wasn't and never had been a violent person, I believed him and instantly felt bad. To be told you'd been verbally and physically abusive while drunk is not the best thing to hear about yourself. Both guilt stricken and ashamed of my actions, I remained in a relationship with someone who had hurt me not once now, but twice. It was against my better judgement and I was ignoring any thoughts about my future wellbeing. On reflection, I attribute this to Aaron's charm, and his ability to flip the situation onto me, so I felt the shame and guilt that he should have been experiencing himself. I will never know if Aaron was aware of his actions, or if they had simply become a way of life. He really did know how to turn an argument or a situation around, to leave you questioning your behaviour, even when you hadn't been the one in the wrong.

LEARNING POINTS: CONTROL AND COERCION

- Your relationship may feel like a

rollercoaster ride. It may be an on-off romance that only the narcissist controls. Don't doubt yourself and your own self-love!

- A narcissist will chip away at your confidence in order to grind you down and control you – this is also known as 'gaslighting'.

- A key trait of a narcissist is that they will panic if you try to leave them. They cannot handle rejection, as Aaron showed when he begged me to stay after his kiss with Julie. As soon as you start to back away, a narcissist will try *that* much harder to keep you in their lives. To make you feel like they have changed, they will love bomb you, saying all the things you wish to hear. Soon enough though, they'll show you that they never actually changed.

- A narcissist thinks they're right about everything, so they will never apologise to you outright. At best, they will simply gloss over what happened with some small signs of remorse.

8

I WILL WALK ON BURNING HOT COALS FOR YOU, AS LONG AS YOU ONLY SERVE ME

A NARCISSIST'S CHARM IS A POWERFUL THING. AND I know this might sound slightly sadistic, coming from someone who has suffered at the hands of it, but it is also oddly beautiful. What a paradox! Following Aaron's blatant betrayal, he went on a charm offensive and pulled out all the stops to keep me from walking. I cared so deeply for him that I didn't look beyond his surface behaviour. I guess you could argue that I'd fallen in love with a man who didn't actually exist.

Seeing someone struggling turns on the Mother Teresa in me, which is perhaps another reason why I didn't see the relationship for what it was. Our partnership became very one sided, as Aaron had a hold over me, one which I believe he played on during our years together. Perhaps even on our first meeting, he recognised that I would be feeling lonely after returning from Australia. Without a home, I had to completely rebuild my life from scratch. What a perfect time for Aaron to become my knight in shining armour. Perhaps he chose to deceive me from the outset, with only his own selfish goals in mind. Maybe he viewed me as someone who needed to be looked after or saved, both of which would have made him feel important. So many times, Aaron said to me, "Lovina, I would walk on burning hot coals for you." As long as he believed that he had my complete focus, I was safe.

When I'm with someone, I give myself unconditionally: my heart, soul, time and emotions. I was wholly devoted to Aaron and his needs, and I asked for nothing in return. As long as he was growing stronger post his divorce then that was good enough for me. To this day, I don't think that Aaron had any idea of the difficult self-healing work I had put myself through during the five years before we met, but it would be this that would ultimately save me from our toxic partnership. But going back to eight months in, all Aaron could see was my longing to have someone in my life.

At twenty-six, I was feeling ready to settle down, and I believed I could do this with Aaron. After years of working on myself, I finally felt whole and had been able to deal with the pain of losing my mum at the age of 18. I'd learned to love myself and to always see the world for the beauty it has to offer, whatever my circumstances might be. My biological clock was also ticking loudly, with my desire to be married with a child at its strongest. I told Aaron early on in our relationship about my wish to be a mum, but irrespective of this, I naturally chose to love and look after his children as if they were my own. From day one of meeting them, I treated them well, and to this day still do. Charlie even called me mum a few times, though I never consciously tried to replace Anne. You only get one mum, and that bond is so, so special. It was clear that Aaron's children already had a loving mother in their lives, but this was sometimes difficult for them to see through the mess of the divorce. Unfortunately, Aaron and Anne chose to imprint their opinions of each other onto the precious, fragile minds of their offspring. I witnessed Aaron doing this many times.

By the spring of 2006, it was obvious to all my friends that I had committed for life to Aaron and his children. My father taught me never to opt out of my responsibilities and to always see them through. On reflection, this is why the relationship was totally imbalanced from the outset. I was being charmed by the best snake charmer in the world. My friends were similarly fooled by Aaron's apparent love for me. He spoke fondly of me to others, and he seemed so genuine.

The summer of that year is imprinted on my memory. The month of July marks the anniversary of the passing of my dear mother, so I always take time out to just be. This year was different, as another life-changing moment was about to occur. I can remember it so clearly, as if it were only yesterday. I called my dad, Daniel, as I did every day, and he informed me that he'd just been taken to hospital. He explained that during a routine blood pressure check at the doctors, he had coughed up some blood. His GP had had no choice but to send him to A&E in an ambulance. I was at Aaron's and immediately told him what had happened. He didn't hesitate in offering to drive me to the hospital in London. I recall an overwhelming feeling of loss come over me, as I realised my dad was going to die and that I wouldn't have long left with him on this earthly plane. Before we set off, I went to the bathroom and cried and cried. I hadn't wanted to show my vulnerable side to Aaron. After all, I'd been busy looking out for him, too. His skin was rather jaundiced, he was shaky and most days he looked tired. I didn't want him to be worried about me.

All thoughts about Aaron's wellbeing left me when I saw my dear dad lying in his hospital bed looking so helpless. As I sat with him, I began to ponder what a gentleman he was. A real 'man's man', he was kind, generous and forthright. He'd never been one to suffer fools, and he spoke his mind, but if anyone was in trouble, they could rely on him to help; he would give them his last penny. Dad and I enjoyed a good relationship, but it hadn't always been that way. Since Mum's death to cancer, we'd had to work on it. We clashed simply because I looked and acted so much like my mother. At times, Dad found it difficult to be in my company without getting upset.

My mind drifted back to the room, as a doctor came crashing in with the results of some tests. "Mr Starr, we've found a shadow on both your lungs and further investigations must be carried out," he said.

As soon as I heard this, I felt exactly the same sense of loss that I had back at Aaron's, when Dad told me he'd been rushed to hospital. I knew my father had cancer and was extremely sick; I could feel it in my entire being. However, I had to keep it together for his sake, until a diagnosis was formally made.

I was processing all this when my phone suddenly rang, making me jump. It was my cousin, Natasha, calling to say that my auntie, Shirley – my mother's sister-in-law – was nearing the end of her life and that it would be wise to go and see her sooner rather than later. She was in a coma and I needed to go and say my goodbyes. This was one of the few days that I felt completely cherished by Aaron in my time of need. He offered to drive me to see my auntie there and then. So, once we were satisfied that Dad would be comfortable for the night, we left for Shirley's care home in Northampton. As we drove, all I could think about was the family members I had lost to date. We'd suffered a lot of loss already in my family. As well as losing my mum, I'd lost five aunties, five uncles and four cousins.

Now, two of the four remaining members of my immediate family were seriously ill. Growing up, my Auntie Shirley had been more like a grandmother to me. She had married my Uncle Jim when my mum, who was eighteen years younger than him, was just a toddler, and the newlyweds had helped to bring her up. When I came along, she'd been hugely involved in my life, too. What an unexpected day of sorrow it was.

When we arrived at the care home, I felt my tummy drop and thought I was going to be sick. Gathering myself, I left Aaron in the car to go in and see my auntie alone. I didn't want to introduce him to my family under such sad circumstances. I remember entering the room and seeing my cousin Natasha beside my auntie's bed. I sat with her and held her hand while I reminisced about the past and how much love and kindness she'd shown me. Yet again, it struck me just how precious life is, and that it should always be lived in the moment.

As I left the home and walked towards the car, I knew I'd never see my auntie again. But as I climbed into the passenger seat, Aaron didn't even ask me how I was. We were both silent as he drove us to our accommodation, an entire converted barn to ourselves for the night.

Aaron had taken it upon himself to make the booking, and initially I'd seen his gesture as extremely kind and thoughtful. I failed to see the bigger picture, which was that rather than driving home, Aaron had wanted to go somewhere and have a drink. Once again, his own needs were at the forefront of his decision-making. As the evening unfolded, Aaron tried hard to seduce me. It had been an awfully painful and emotional day for me, but instead of asking how I was, his focus turned inwards, to his own needs. Given that I had just said goodbye to my precious auntie, the last thing I wanted was to make love. Yet I still chose to focus on the good in Aaron. After all, he'd booked the accommodation and dropped everything to drive me hundreds of miles to London and then Northampton. In retrospect, I failed to admit to myself that he had not once considered my emotional needs.

LEARNING POINTS: ALL ABOUT ME, MYSELF AND I

- A true narcissist believes that they are special and unique, and that they can only be understood by other special and unique individuals. They will walk on burning hot coals for you, as long as you give them constant praise and admiration.
- The narcissist in your life will display a lack of empathy towards you and your emotionally sensitive situations. Meanwhile, they can be great on a logistical and practical level, as Aaron showed when

my family members became suddenly ill and he ferried me between the hospital and care home. This quality can disguise their lack of empathy.

- A narcissist may often do something that seems incredibly supportive, such as when Aaron booked the room for me, but in essence they are still putting their own needs first.

9

PUTTING THE NEEDS OF OTHERS
BEFORE YOUR OWN

SPENDING TIME WITH THE CHILDREN FILLED ME WITH delight, as I was able to put their needs before my own. Charlie and Arabella always came to us with an abundance of sadness. I attributed this to them bearing witness to their parents' arguments and acrimonious divorce. I tried to allow them the much-needed space to be children again, and to unlock their inner joy. I find I can be my authentic self with little people, and from the outset, Charlie and I formed a unique spiritual bond. I could read his soul, and the struggles he faced were clear for me to see.

I was there for Arabella a hundred per cent, too. I felt compelled by unseen forces to help them both, and to ensure they always felt safe and secure. Arabella often came from her mother's house in a state of upset, and then Aaron would harp on about what Anne had done to him. He was hurting, but as time passed, seeing him put the children in that painful situation made me look upon him differently. Yes, it was hard for him, as most days Anne attacked him over email, but instead of letting it go, or calmly responding, he would react and be just as vicious in his replies. When we were together as a family, I tried so hard to shield the cherubs from their dad's anger and pain. I planned all our trips, as Aaron was busy battling his anxiety and mental health problems. I was happy to take the reins because fixing and healing is what I do best. I never allowed Aaron to spend long periods of time alone with the children, where he might dwell on his ex and rant to them about her. I knew how damaging it was to their emotional wellbeing, and looking back, his behaviour was incredibly selfish.

They came to visit shortly after my aunt had passed away and Dad had been diagnosed with stage four lung cancer, as deep down I'd known he would be. They proved the perfect distraction, allowing me to escape from all my pent-up emotions. I felt so protective over them, especially Charlie. I attributed this to our godly bond, as well as to him being viewed as the black sheep of the family. I believe that you meet people in your life for a reason, season or a lifetime, and I felt the children's paths had crossed mine for all three of those things. As it was the summer holidays and we had more time together than usual, I planned a trip to Croatia. I was really looking forward to it, but Aaron was anxious, as he wasn't sure if he would be able to cope. Charlie was already staying with us, and Arabella came over a few days before we were due to fly out. It was to be our first holiday abroad as a family unit, and I can remember my elation at spending quality time getting to know Aaron's world on a deeper level. And what a holiday it would turn out to be.

To kick off our trip, we all enjoyed the business class lounge at Heathrow Airport, with all the delicious food and various drinks on offer. I realised then that trying to keep Aaron's heavy drinking from the children would not be an easy task, and I began to secretly pray that all would be OK. The glasses of pink champagne flowed, and Aaron seemed to be handling it all too well. I only consumed two glasses before I put on my 'mum hat'. My overriding instinct was to make sure Aaron's children were taken care of, which was far more important to me than getting the most out of the free bar.

Now, I can say with certainty that Aaron loves his children more than anything else. His feelings for them are probably the closest he has come to such strong emotions, and he totally dotes on them. I could see from observing him with them how extremely proud he was to be their father. But beyond this, I could also see a broken man using drink to fight his demons and past hurts. The trip proved to be a real eye opener, as it's when I truly realised I was dating an addict. I watched him kick back the pink champagne as if it was orange squash. No doubt aware of how this looked, he sent Arabella and me off to buy something nice from the airport shops. With Charlie occupied by his phone, this left him in peace to drink even more.

On the plane, we were all seated in business class. Aaron sat next to Arabella behind me, while I was with Charlie. The food was out of this world. It was standard practice for Aaron to fly either business or first class, but for the rest of us it was a real treat, and we were all super excited and in awe of the service. The chicken curry and chocolate dessert we dined on were truly yummy and served with silver cutlery rather than plastic. Aaron and I enjoyed more pink champagne as we bantered with the cabin staff. At this point, Aaron was still love bombing me and duly put on a show. He looked in the shopping section of the inflight magazine and repeatedly asked me if I wanted anything.

"Thank you, but I don't need things in order to be happy," I reassured him. Unable to shut him up, I visited the toilet, hoping he'd put the magazine down. When I returned, Aaron was holding up a bag.

"I hope your dad hasn't got me anything," I said to Charlie.

The boy simply smiled and looked from me to the bag, urging me to open it. Aaron had purchased for me some beautiful and most unexpected gifts, including a Pandora charm, which represented family, to go with the bracelet he'd given me for my birthday back in

May. There was another box with two expensive bracelets in it. Looking back, I don't believe he gave me the gifts with any real sentiment. I turned to thank him, not knowing what to say other than, "You really shouldn't have."

"You are part of our family now, sweetie," Aaron responded, while taking a sip of his third gin and tonic.

Aaron continued to enjoy the free bar for the rest of the relatively short flight. The next time I turned around to check in on Arabella, who was a nervous flyer, I saw that Aaron had completely passed out, with his head resting on the seat in front of him. Luckily, Arabella looked content. She was cuddling into her daddy whilst holding onto her penguin teddy for dear life. I began to wonder how much Aaron drank on a daily basis. Despite my concern, I didn't want to ruin the holiday and vowed to keep my thoughts to myself.

After landing in Croatia, I had to get through customs and arrange a car to drive us to our accommodation – all with two tired cherubs and a drunk boyfriend in tow. Luckily, I was blessed with finding a taxi relatively quickly, and soon we were off to our hotel, a fantastic holiday complex at the top of a hill. It was a fabulous home away from home, with the added bonus of guaranteed sunshine. We had a fun-filled week consisting of time at the beach and around the hotel swimming pool. The sunset balcony barbecues went down a treat, too. I wouldn't be able to fault the holiday if it weren't for Aaron's alcohol addiction rearing its ugly head, as I had feared it might. After our evening meal, Arabella, tired from all the play and sunshine, would go to bed at a reasonable time. Charlie, being older, asked to stay up and watch a film or play games with us, but all Aaron wanted was to sit on the balcony with me and drink wine all night long. For the first half of the holiday, I did just that. After all, it was our break together, too. But being someone who is into fitness and rarely drinks, as the week wore on, I was less willing to compromise in order to adapt to Aaron's way of life. Instead, after the first bottle had been drunk, I chose to have a cup of herbal tea instead. This triggered something in Aaron. The first time I did it, he made it clear that he didn't like me sitting there with him without a proper drink in my hand.

"Why do you have to be so boring? You are ruining our time together," he said, as I put the kettle on.

"I just fancy some tea. You know how my tummy plays up when I drink a lot of wine."

"It is always excuses with you, Lovina."

To this day, I will never understand how a beautiful, hot summer's evening on a balcony, with music and stars shining brightly could be spoilt, but it was.

"Do you do it purposely?"

"What do you mean, Aaron, do what purposely?"

"Try and take away the fun. You are boring and you think you are important."

"Aaron, what are you talking about? I just wanted to have some peppermint tea to calm my tummy down from the acidity of the wine. That's all, lovely."

"I am not your lovely! You are mean to me. You choose not to sit with me and drink. You are evil! You are ruining my holiday! You are like their mother and trying to control what I do."

"Aaron, I am nothing like Anne. In fact, I'm the complete opposite of her."

"No!" Aaron shouted. He stood up, loomed over me and wagged his index finger. "You are her! You are always making out that you are better than me for not drinking as much. You blame me for enjoying life. You take and spend my money like it's water. She did, too."

I couldn't understand why I was being blamed for his ex's behaviour. I absorbed the hurtful words and allowed myself to feel bad for not drinking more alcohol.

"You should have stayed at home rather than coming here and spoiling my holiday," Aaron continued. "You are evil, pure evil!"

Aaron became so intoxicated and unbearable to be with that I was unable to sit and have a coherent conversation with him. For the rest of the holiday, his intoxicated outbursts made me shut down a little more each day. By the end of the trip, I was being emotionally and physically distant towards him, for my own protection. I did not wish to be close with him on an intimate level. This wound Aaron up even more, and he would tell me how ungrateful I was, as he had paid for our holiday together. All this when it was actually me who had covered the flights and accommodation. How can someone emotionally and verbally abuse a loved one like that, and for no good reason, and then simply switch on the romance, expecting them to reciprocate? I loved Aaron and tried to be close with him, but at times I actually believed what he had been drilling into my subconscious mind. I would go to bed upset and in tears, while wondering why he would get so hammered and treat me so badly. I came to the conclusion that he still had issues with his ex and her lack of affection towards him. I gave continuous excuses for my atrocious treatment, and I stayed in the relationship. I thought it was love. How wrong was I. In fairness, I had never experienced being with an alcoholic before, let alone a narcissist. At a time in my life when I needed to be wanted, I thought this man cherished me. I can see now that I may have been emotionally off balance and feeling at a root level that I needed someone like Aaron in order to have a family life. Loss and grief can knock you off balance, allowing you to be blindsided.

After returning from Croatia, the children had a few more days with us before going back to their mother. I resumed my work and went to see one of my life-coaching clients. Afterwards, I turned on my phone to see that I had at least six missed calls and texts from Aaron asking me to go over to his. I drove straight there and found him in the kitchen pacing up and down. I asked him what had happened, and he said that I needed to know what his son had just done. He called the boy down and continued his pacing, as Charlie told us how he had called the police to ask for help with his mother and grandad. Apparently, they had told him that from now on, he would only be allowed to see Aaron every other weekend, and if he visited his house at any other times, they would all get into trouble with the police. Charlie explained that when he questioned his mum and grandad about this, they told him that Aaron had signed a 'contract' agreeing to the arrangement. The poor lad couldn't believe his dad would do such a thing and had called 101 for advice.

The 101 responder had asked to speak to Aaron, as Charlie had said that he did not wish to go home to his mum's with Arabella later that day. What a mess! I really felt for Charlie, as he seemed somewhat afraid of his mum, a feeling that was no doubt fuelled by Aaron's obvious hatred of her. Nevertheless, I couldn't help but think the worst of Anne. Charlie asked if he could move in with Aaron on a permanent basis. His dad explained that this wouldn't be possible due to his working hours. At this point, Charlie turned around, looked me straight in the eye and said, "Lovina can look after me."

I was overwhelmed. A 13-year-old boy, whom I had not known for very long, was asking me to care for him, when there were already cracks in my relationship with his father. The way he'd called 101 and personally asked for my help really pulled at my heart strings. I knew the responsibility would be huge, and that I had to consider his mother's feelings, but I couldn't just say no. I tried to discuss this delicate matter with Aaron, but every time I brought the subject up, he'd say, "Anne never considered my feelings when she moved the children out while I was away."

Once again, I was being dragged into their battle. Still, I felt drawn to helping Charlie with his request; not to hurt Aaron's ex-wife or to side with Aaron, but to come to the aid of the person who seemed to be suffering the most.

LEARNING POINTS: REACTING RATHER THAN RESPONDING

- When they feel they have been exposed, narcissists will lash out. They can be extremely vicious in their response to emotionally demanding situations, especially ones that they cannot handle due to their lack of empathy.

- Self*ish* opposed to self*less*. A narcissist always displays an exaggerated sense of self-importance and will exploit others without guilt or shame.
- Mirroring is a trap a narcissist will often lay. Lacking a healthy relationship with themselves, they will come to rely on your feedback, and the feedback of the other people in their lives, to provide them with a self-image. This reflection tells them that they exist and also helps to define them. Without it, they simply do not know who they are.

10

GRIEF IS THE LAST ACT OF LOVE WE CAN GIVE TO THOSE WE CARE ABOUT

IF YOU'D TOLD ME BACK IN 1998, WHEN MY MOTHER died, that my dad would eventually become my new rock, I would have told you that there was more chance of me winning the lottery.

You see, Daniel struggled to cope following Mum's death and went through a phase of drinking in the day, blaring out Queen at all hours and shouting at me for no reason. For a while, my brother Johnny and I were on a real emotional rollercoaster ride with him, as he took his anger out on us. But with time, understanding, self-reflective practice and healing, we made amends and were able to be there for each other, just like my mother and I had been.

By the end of the summer of 2006, I was living with Aaron in his former family home and Charlie's guardian. I was also running back and forth to London to be my dad's end-of-life helper. My mother had always taught me that it's tough at the top, and she wasn't wrong – mothers seldom are. They're wise owls, the lot of them.

The next two months were both traumatic and intense. Looking back, I was giving my all to whoever needed my unconditional love. As well as taking care of my dying dad, I had stepped up to nurture Charlie, was keeping Aaron on track with his work and looking after Arabella whenever she came to visit – all whilst Aaron continued to drink to hide from his anxiety and emotional pain. Throughout my life, I have given without expecting anything in return, but at that time I felt so very alone. Watching my dad losing his battle was like seeing my mum going through her fight against cancer all over again. It was so painful and a true test of my strength, resilience and ability to handle loss. My life partner just wasn't capable of providing me with the empathetic support I so needed. Life can appear cruel at certain times, and yet it can also be beautiful. What I endured with Aaron, as horrific as it felt at times, was because of a choice that came from the heart. I'd decided to love a broken, wounded man while knowing that I would never have the relationship I had initially envisaged. As you'll discover, the good news is that once you become aware of what's going on and feel strong enough to act, you can choose to leave such a relationship. You will respond for your own greater good.

During this difficult time, my intuition was guiding

me and telling me that being an island wasn't the way forward, and that I needed some support. Sometimes, a girl just needs her daddy to listen to her, and mine did this for me, despite his own immense physical pain. I will never forget our chat about what I had endured through seeing my mum get sick at such a young age, and how proud he was of me. All my dad ever wanted was to see his little girl settled with a family of her own.

Unburdening myself to Dad instantaneously lifted a weight off my shoulders. I explained about Aaron's alcoholism and controlling behaviour. Lately, he had switched from drinking secretly to openly boozing, while I took care of Charlie. Aaron seemed to have stopped caring and didn't think to hide his empty bottles from the children. I explained how although I wasn't scared of Aaron physically, as I knew he would never lash out, his drinking and verbal abuse often drove me to tears and I felt vulnerable around him. At the end of the evening, I would purposely leave Aaron drinking downstairs in the lounge, listening loudly to Paolo Nutini or rewatching *Jools' Annual Hootenanny*, while I cried myself to sleep upstairs.

"I often wonder what I have done to deserve all this," I admitted.

I can recall my dear dad looking at me with a concerned expression on his face. I went onto explain how Aaron often called me by his ex-wife's name. I felt as if he was using my presence to re-enact their volatile past life together. I reflected how in some ways Aaron's behaviour mirrored Dad's after he lost mum. He had managed to pull himself through it, and I wondered whether Aaron could do the same. I thought how his rather complex childhood issues, coupled with his relationship with his ex-wife may have knocked his self-esteem, to the point where he felt unworthy of love. Could that explain why he regularly lashed out at me, because he was jealous that I was holding everything together when he couldn't?

Two weeks later, I went to visit Dad in hospital, and he demanded that I take him home, as he was, in his own words, "Going to die at five o' clock."

It was midday Saturday, so the hospital had on a skeleton staff, with no doctors available to discharge him until Monday. But Dad said he'd never forgive me if I didn't get him out. "If you truly are a caring daughter then you will get me home to be with your mother when I pass," he said. "I will not die here alone. I want to be in my own home when they come for me."

I forgave the harshness of his manner, as I knew he was in unbearable pain and was also scared about passing to the other side. I spoke to the hospital management team and eventually managed to get him discharged. An ambulance was assigned to take him home, and I followed in my car. As soon as we'd got him into his bed, he asked me to call Aaron and Charlie to come over and say their farewells. It was now one o'clock, which meant we were only four hours away from the time when Dad had said he would pass. Luckily, I got hold of Aaron straight away and he headed over with Charlie, whom Dad had taken quite a shine to.

Once Dad had said what he wanted to say to Charlie, he asked him to go and wait outside in the car. He then called Aaron into the bedroom. I went to go, thinking I should leave the men to it, but quite sternly, Dad asked me to remain in the room and to sit next to him on the bed. Meanwhile, Aaron took position at the foot of the bed.

"You're a good man, he started, "but if you don't move on from your ex-wife and hesitate over marrying my daughter and having a child with her then I've told her to get the hell out of Dodge!"

Aaron looked rather shocked, but simply replied, "Yes, Daniel, I promise I won't let her down."

My dad went on to talk to him about his drinking, reassuring him that he was better than the way he was currently behaving, and that his past didn't define his future. My dad may not have been a psychologist or a psychiatrist, but he was pretty clued up and wise. Aaron appeared to be taking onboard what he was saying.

Once Dad had said his piece, he told Aaron he loved him and to look after what he had with me. He then ushered him out of the room. Aaron and Charlie left, and we waited for my brother to arrive. Dad made it past his five pm departure time fully coherent and very much alive. Not wishing to burden us any further, he then insisted that my brother and I leave. I really wanted to stay but chose to respect his wishes. I went to join Aaron at his brother's house. We'd decided to stay there for the night, as it was only a thirty-minute drive from Dad's. I spent the rest of the evening trying to switch off, but I was troubled by the fact that Dad was on his own. Aaron spent the evening drinking wine with his brother. At midnight, when it was time to go to bed, I burst out crying and said, "I won't be able to sleep knowing my dad is by himself. I must be with him for his passing."

"I've been drinking, so I can't drive," Aaron said rather angrily.

"Then I'll go on my own," I replied.

"No, don't do that. I'll have some coffee, sober up a bit and then take you."

Thank goodness for small mercies. I waited patiently for Aaron to make and consume several cups of black coffee, and then we headed back to Dad's.

When we arrived, I popped my head round his bedroom door. He was sound asleep and breathing heavily. I noticed that he was leaning against the wall, and I figured he must have fallen asleep while looking at a picture of Mum, as it was directly in his eyeline. This gave me so much joy to see. I ventured further into his room and whispered, "Dad, I am here. I couldn't leave you, although you asked me to. Sorry. I love you. Sleep soundly. I give you permission to go and be with Mum."

I let him be and went to the lounge, where Aaron and I set up camp on an old single mattress. The lounge was next to Dad's room, and I wanted to be close to him in case he needed anything in the night. Aaron snuggled into me and held me tight. "Sweetie, it's all right, I am here with you. I love you," he said.

Comforted, I fell asleep in his arms. I can remember this being one of the times when I was truly grateful to have Aaron there for me, as it was such an emotionally difficult time.

At 5 am, I was woken by something physically nudging me. I bolted upright and shouted out loud, "They've taken him."

Aaron began to stir, as I rushed next door. I could see that Dad's mouth was wide open, his dentures half out. I felt he had died, but slowly walked towards his body to see if his chest was rising. It wasn't. I went back into the lounge, climbed into Aaron's arms and said, "Dad's gone." Then I sobbed and sobbed for what seemed like hours. I was so sad that he'd gone and left, as I loved our chats and times together.

Where there is deep love comes an even deeper grief. After losing my father, I made a conscious choice to sit with my grief, which lasted a good two months. I used the time to reflect on the wise words that Dad had imparted to Aaron and me from his deathbed. During this period of hibernation, I began to identify the cracks in our relationship. For example, how Aaron enjoyed putting me down in order to lift himself up. He fed off compliments, which was a result of his own low self-esteem. During and post my dad's passing, I was party to his lack of empathy. Conversely, his son's empathic nature shined through. Charlie was truly kind and loving towards me during this difficult time in my life, and I will be eternally grateful for the unconditional love he showed me. As a result of this, a stronger bond forged between me and Charlie, alongside a deeper dysfunctional tie to Aaron.

The Christmas of 2006 soon came around to add some joy to my loss. Arabella came to spend the week with us, leaving on Boxing Day, while Charlie chose to spend the rest of the holiday with his dad and me. On New Year's Day, we went for a drive to an idyllic pub in a remote village. We wanted to spend the first day of the new year as a unit. As we ate, we discussed my wish to have a holiday alone with Aaron. What Dad had said to us before his passing was still at the forefront of my mind, and I thought this time would give us the chance to discuss what we wanted from the future, and hopefully get back on track. On top of this, my grief had brought with it a desire to live life to the full and go back to being the free-spirited woman of my early twenties.

For once, Aaron was in agreement and offered to book us a holiday to Jamaica. I was so excited and felt my soul coming alive, as I thought how this might just be the lift I needed. After all, since meeting, Aaron and I had both endured losses of one kind or another.

Forever hopeful and determined to live in joy, I believed 2007 was going to be a time for change and rebirth. However, the holiday wasn't quite going to provide us with the alone time I craved. Charlie refused to go to Anne's for the week we planned to go away. I could see that he needed his father's nurturing during an emotionally difficult teenage time, so I had no issue with him coming with us, as it was the right thing to do. Aaron had come into the relationship with two children, and I'd chosen to accept them from the outset, so I felt it would be wrong of me to object to Charlie coming along. Aaron, on the other hand, was not best pleased and took his annoyance out on me.

One night, he drank copious amounts of alcohol in secret and came upstairs completely intoxicated. He proceeded to try and push me out of the bed several times. "Get out, you whore!" he shouted. "Go and love my son, in his bed, as you clearly love him more than you love me."

I turned the light on so I could look him in the eye and try and reason with him, but he carried on screaming, this time with his face just inches from mine. "You are ruining our relationship. You want Charlie more than you want me. It's disgusting how you flaunt yourself in front of his mates, making them want you."

I was completely shocked by the outburst. Seeing how drunk Aaron was, I dealt with it the best way I knew how – by choosing not to react to his lies. Instead, I said nothing, turned off the light and cuddled into his back until he fell asleep. This was a true light-bulb moment of awareness, as I realised just how deep Aaron's self-hatred ran. I could feel how envious he was of me as a whole and balanced being. Over time, my strength and self-love would continue to remind Aaron of what he lacked, which ultimately led to the demise of our relationship.

LEARNING POINTS: IDENTIFY, ADMIT AND QUESTION

- The first step is to admit to yourself that there are issues in your relationship.
- Secondly, identify that there is more to the imbalance than what is typically faced by couples due to gender differences.
- Thirdly, ask yourself, "Am I being gaslighted?" It is only then that you may begin to wonder, "Am I seeing some narcissistic traits in my partner?"
- After step three, I reached a point where I could recognise situations that I had worked

on with my own clients regarding relationship narcissism.

- I came to see that I loved my whole self a lot more than the narcissist, who was in turn trying to denigrate who I was as a person.

11

CARIBBEAN CHAOS

T HE TIME HAD FINALLY COME FOR OUR HOLIDAY TO THE Caribbean. It was Easter 2007, and I was looking forward to love, romance and lots of fun-filled laughter. What I got was something entirely different. Did you know that a chameleon will always end up showing their true self? Aaron's addictive behaviour and lack of respect and empathy for others came out in full force during our time away. This is when his gaslighting really kicked in and I saw the true depth of his internal wrath and self-esteem issues. What was meant to be a holiday of a lifetime with my loved one was actually a trip to hell that I wouldn't wish on my worst enemy. I don't actually know what was worse, spending the week being constantly belittled and told I was no good, or having to come home and pretend to the world that it was the best holiday ever. The week itself and the days afterwards were extremely challenging, and I found myself close to breaking point several times, both physically and mentally.

My happy-go-lucky character was tested to the limit, but I would not allow what I endured to kill me inside, despite it taking so much out of me. Anyone who has had a narcissist in their life will understand. Had I not been through my own rebirth post reactive depression and anxiety following Dad's death, then Aaron may have actually broken me. I was blessed with my wholeness and faith to get me through, and it's now my mission to help others who are experiencing the same kind of trauma.

Going back to the holiday, the all-inclusive resort Aaron had booked for us was beyond luxurious. The food on offer was varied and fresh and there were daily games and watersports for when you wanted a 'break' from sunbathing. At first, I felt as if I had gone to holiday heaven. The only downside was the man I was with. Due to his drink problem, Aaron should not have been staying somewhere where the booze was on tap. When we'd first met, I'd seen him as someone who was fun, spontaneous, sporty and willing to try anything once. What I witnessed in Jamaica was a man who was more interested in hovering by the poolside bar than spending quality time with the partner who had given him her all. I tried to let it slide, telling myself that his behaviour was down to his job. Stress and pressure were part and parcel of his chosen career, and Aaron wouldn't have had it any other way. He placed materialistic things higher than his own and his loved ones' wellbeing. However, for once I had convinced him to leave his laptop in his room and enjoy his rest time. I was looking forward to trying the watersports with him, indulging in a few cocktails and kissing as we watched the sunset. What did I get? Aaron drinking from the moment the bars opened at 10 am to when they closed in the early hours of the morning.

At the start of each day, Charlie and I enjoyed the company of a relatively happy Aaron, who would join in with some of the sports. Yet fast forward to the evening, after he had consumed copious amounts of alcohol, and what we got was the polar opposite; a verbally abusive, unhappy, bitter Aaron. He even called me a c*nt in front of his son. This wasn't something I had signed up for when I entered into the relationship. Not for the first time, I wondered where the man I had fallen in love with was.

Despite everything, I do have some fond memories of the good times we did manage to spend together. Charlie and I always took part in the midday volleyball pool session, along with the resort's other guests. Sometimes, Aaron would join in, but more often than not he would slip away to cheer us on by the poolside bar. Even during our darkest times together, I could always see his good side. I felt the kindness in his heart and soul, but I believed it had become overshadowed by his past trauma and hurts. I felt he needed the intervention of a professional to help him deal with them. I didn't think for one moment that I could 'fix' him, but I did live in the naive hope that he cared for and loved me enough to at some point seek professional help. Unfortunately, this day never came during our time together and I was forced to witness the further unravelling of my broken man.

On most evenings after dinner, Charlie and I would go up to our room so that we didn't have to endure Aaron's intense post-drinking mood swings. Although I wanted to spend time with my partner, I also had to protect Charlie's emotional wellbeing. I calmly took the abuse that Aaron hurled at me over dinner, before removing Charlie from the situation. I wanted to lessen his exposure to his dysfunctional dad. As the week wore on, my heart really did start to break for Charlie. Unfortunately, he got to witness the dark side of the man he clearly doted on. To this day, I still feel awful over what he witnessed during that holiday. Back at home, I was able to implement strategies to shield him, but in Jamaica this wasn't possible. When we returned to England, I made a secret call to Alcoholics Anonymous for advice and realised that Aaron was what's termed a 'functional alcoholic'.

Our final day of the holiday was dreadful, as I became physically unwell from overexposure to negativity and stress. I was passing black, blood-stained stools and felt and looked a wreck. I realised that if I didn't improve soon, I wouldn't make it through the ninety-minute coach journey to the airport. This was one of the rare times in my life when I've suffered from stress-induced IBS. Although I experienced severe diarrhoea after my dad passed away, this was far, far worse. Mentally, I wasn't myself, either. I felt anxious and underconfident, and I had taken to biting my nails. I wondered if I was being oversensitive, and if any of Aaron's outbursts had been my fault. I guess it was natural to doubt myself, as Aaron kept telling me that I was either wrong or doing wrong. I can remember constantly apologising, which I know now was a result of the gaslighting. Aaron was starting to break me down.

On top of everything, Charlie had emetophobia, which is a fear of either being sick or seeing other people being sick. He knew that I was unwell and started to panic. The anxiety of my impending sickness, even though I didn't actually feel nauseous, enhanced Charlie's condition. It was all psychosomatic with him. Just hours before we were due to depart the resort for the airport, the two of us were in a right pickle.

To be fair on Aaron, being an unemotional sort meant that he was a good problem solver. Not wishing to miss our flight home, which would have incurred extra costs, he took the lead and sourced a helicopter to take us from the hotel complex to the airport, all in time for our flight back to the UK. While Charlie was excited by this change in schedule, I was rather fearful. However, knowing that my bowels wouldn't last the long coach ride, I was grateful to Aaron for coming up with an alternative. His helpfulness left me feeling overwhelmed and turned my thoughts away from all the bad stuff that had happened over the course of the week. On reflection, this seems crazy given the alcohol-induced abuse I had endured.

LEARNING POINTS: CAN YOU MAINTAIN A RELATIONSHIP WITH A NARCISSIST?

- First, turn your focus inwards and ask yourself the following questions: "Am I worthy? Do I love who I am?" If you do choose to stay with and survive a narcissist, self-awareness and self-love are key.
- Most narcissists don't have many, if any, healthy or lasting relationships. Some may achieve what is outwardly perceived as 'success,' but this will be at the expense of their personal life. It can be lonely at the top.
- I firmly believe that if a narcissist chooses to seek professional help, their relationship could last long-term. Boundaries will need to be set and their other half must understand who they are and maintain self-

love, as the partnership will continue to be both emotionally and psychologically exhausting. After all, in my humble experience, narcissists can't help but drain all the life and spirit from their partners.

12

THE ONLY PERSON YOU CAN
CONTROL, AT BEST, IS YOURSELF

WE WERE DUE TO MOVE TO A NEW HOUSE IN A neighbouring village, and the completion date for the sale coincided with my girls' holiday to Fuerteventura and my 28th birthday celebrations. I couldn't help wondering whether Aaron had arranged this purposely to scupper my plans. In the three days leading up to my departure, all he did was rant at me for going away. I had never been one to shirk my responsibilities, and I wasn't about to start now, so rather than preparing for my trip by shopping, being pampered and packing, I loaded up box after box of Aaron's belongings. There isn't another woman I know who would have put up with that kind of treatment, unless they were living with or in fear of a narcissist.

The abuse that Aaron hurled at me for going on a prearranged holiday was unbelievable. Again, I put it down to his insecurities. I had become accustomed to making excuses for his inappropriate behaviour, as he often spouted unkind untruths about me to others. I was longing to spend some time away from him on a beach far, far away. I chose to help Aaron pack up and move his entire life, without any complaints, and yet he repaid me with nastiness.

"You're going away and leaving me to move house," he spat. "That's hardly supportive. You don't love me – you only love yourself."

The trouble is, I could see the man that Aaron could become if he simply chose to do the work on himself. As always in our relationship, I also felt I had to stick around to help his children. I loved them dearly, especially as they were the innocent ones in all of this.

Whilst I was away, Aaron was due to have both Arabella and Charlie staying with him. Knowing that he would need some support, I spoke to his sister-in-law and asked if it would be OK if they visited her and Aaron's brother at the weekend. I could then relax, knowing that the kids wouldn't be spending the whole time alone with their alcoholic dad. His sister-in-law was such a loving, kind and thoughtful lady, and she did not hesitate to help me.

Now, you may think that it was dangerous for me to confide in her, as her loyalties lay with Aaron, but she was her own person and chose to see people for who they really were. I loved her approach to life, and I was blessed to have her help from afar. I felt reassured that I could go off and relax with the ladies, before returning to help Aaron unpack at the new house. I knew he would have been stressed by looking after his cherubs in the midst of the move, yet he was still resentful towards me for stepping into help. This man really did know how to emotionally drain me, which made me all the more determined to focus only on myself while in Fuerteventura. I just wanted to sit on a sunbed all day, speak to no one and recharge, rejuvenate and rebalance my soul. Looking back, this became my survival strategy. I would often escape to have some me time and regain my perspective on situations, especially when Aaron was accusing me of all manner of things.

My weekend away could not have come around soon enough. A taxi was picking me up at 3.30 am, as we had an early flight from Gatwick Airport. I was up and ready by 3 am, stupidly hoping to cuddle Aaron before my departure, but I didn't even get a "see you later". Instead, he remained in bed, apparently asleep. I left feeling a tad guilty. However, within thirty minutes of me leaving, Aaron chose to love bomb me with incessant texts proclaiming his undying love for his sweetie and asking me to stay safe whilst I was away. I thought that maybe he had reflected on how awful he had been towards me recently. Maybe he had sensed that I was no longer happy or in awe of him and had decided that it wouldn't be a good time to lose me. Going through a divorce and moving home are supposedly two of the most stressful things you can go through in life. Aaron was experiencing them concurrently. While I chose to make excuses for his behaviour towards me, I was also forming some boundaries.

From the moment I met the other ladies at 'stupid o' clock' in the morning, the champagne flowed in the airport bar. This long weekend was providing me with the much-needed fun and frolics that had been missing from my life over the last year, and I was looking forward to indulging in the things I love – laughter, flat whites, time with friends and, of course, meditative time with Jesus.

After landing and checking in at our hotel, we were able to hit the sunbeds by early afternoon, relax and enjoy the rays. As it was an all-inclusive hotel, we also took full advantage of the cocktails. It was a chance for me to unwind and fully be myself. I didn't have to be wary of Aaron drinking too much and behaving badly in front of Charlie. Just thinking of this made me recall how, while packing for the house move, I'd found countless empty wine bottles and beer cans hidden in his conservatory.

Not that my friends knew anything about what was happening behind the scenes of my relationship. I never thought to confide in them. I wasn't embarrassed, but I guess I didn't want them to judge the man I loved and had chosen to be with. Since Dad's passing, I had been keeping all the pain and hurt to myself, even though, six months on, I was still struggling with the loss. Aaron didn't want to know about my emotions. When I tried to talk to him about them, he would either change the subject or walk away.

Ironically, it was Dad I wanted to talk things over with. Before his passing, I would check in with him every day, and he and I would discuss Aaron and how I was feeling. He had been such an amazing support and I felt his absence acutely. He would continuously praise me for sticking by Aaron and not giving up on him or my responsibility to Charlie. Not having him around to confide in now was really starting to take its toll and affect my ability to cope. I can clearly remember thinking, whilst soaking up the sun, that perhaps it would be good to open up to Kelly. But Aaron had convinced me that talking about us to anyone outside of our home would be a form of betrayal. Narcissists tend to have a strong desire to control the narrative and how other people perceive them. They hate criticism and never present their real selves. Aaron had drilled it into me that he was always right. In his mind, there was either a winner or a loser, and he was invariably the former.

Despite all this, over the course of our break, I did share with Kelly some snippets of what was happening, including Aaron's alcoholism and our not-so romantic holiday to Jamaica. She advised me not to be a slave to my phone and to hold off from replying to

Aaron's numerous text messages. After all, I was on a girls' holiday and this was my time for rest and recuperation.

After a day of me not texting, Aaron got really upset with me. That evening, he phoned and told me I was selfish and out of order. It turned out he hadn't even bothered to go round to his brother's house, as I'd arranged with his sister-in-law, to give him some respite from looking after the kids. He was on speaker phone, which meant that Charlie and Arabella could hear him. "You left us to move house and deal with everything," he yelled yet again.

I was stunned and didn't know how to respond. Coming off the phone, I could see Kelly looking at me from the other side of our shared bedroom. She'd picked up enough to be appalled at Aaron's behaviour and explained that her husband would never 'check in' on her whilst she was on holiday with the girls. This was her time away from the family environment and from being a mother and a wife. Why couldn't Aaron afford me that, too?

For the rest of my break, I couldn't help but question why Aaron had been so cruel to me, especially in front of the children. I felt bullied and believed that Aaron must have done it to boost his low self-esteem.

On the other side of the coin, my trip was a real ego booster. My plan was to top up on my Vitamin D and relax with the ladies, but I couldn't help but notice that I wasn't without some admiring glances from the opposite sex. On day three, a lovely young man from Birmingham approached me in the breakfast queue and introduced himself. His name was Richard, he was in his early 20s, and he had a thick Brummie accent and some crazy sunburn going on. He actually resembled Rudolph the reindeer, and I had no issue in telling him this, either. Despite feeling embarrassed at being blatantly chatted up so early in the morning, I actually felt a bit of the old, light-hearted Lovina returning.

"I can see you must be trouble," Richard coyly remarked.

I escaped entering a full-blown conversation with this handsome stranger by scurrying back to my table. I immediately told Kelly what had happened. I somehow felt guilty. Again, it was a misplaced emotion, as I hadn't actually done anything wrong.

That day by the pool, I tried to understand why I felt such guilt over chatting with another man. I realised it was because I could hear Aaron's disapproving voice in my head, telling me how inappropriate my behaviour was.

Later, I could see Richard staring at me from his sunbed opposite. Was I tempted? Well, I was certainly flattered. A fit-looking, younger guy had approached me and been both kind and complimentary. At the same time, my supposedly loving partner was hurling abuse down the phone at me and sending me nasty texts.

The trip was a real game changer for me, as I realised just how stressed I was at home compared to the freedom and fun I experienced while away. I loved Aaron and still wanted a future with him, and maybe even a child of our own, but I had given so much of myself already, only to be told how useless I was. Having just moved into our first home together, I wondered how things would go when I returned. Our lives were already so intertwined.

Our flight back to the UK was delayed, meaning I wouldn't be arriving home until the early hours. I texted Aaron and asked him to wait up for me, as I was yet to get a key for the new house cut. He was clearly unhappy when he answered the door. He looked at me with no emotion whatsoever and then just went back to bed. He gave me nothing to suggest that he had missed me or wanted to welcome me into our new home. I came in, got undressed and climbed straight into bed, cuddling up to Aaron to show how much I had missed him. "Leave me alone, Lovina," he said. "I am still upset with you and I want to go to sleep. Not all of us can afford to go gallivanting about for days on end."

What a great way to spend our first night together in our new home, I thought to myself. I couldn't hold back the tears, which were streaming endlessly down my cheeks. I decided it was best not to respond, so I rolled over, away from him, and tried to get to sleep.

From the moment we woke up the next day until the time we went to bed the following evening, I never heard the end of it. Aaron constantly picked on me, teasing me about all the boxes he had unpacked whilst I was enjoying myself with the girls. Aaron then refused to celebrate my birthday with me, as I had already marked the occasion with my friends. He could be odd like that. For instance, if I said I'd seen a film, Aaron would refuse to watch it again with me – no matter who I'd seen it with the first time. Back then, this actually made me wonder if he might be autistic. However, I have since learned how closely some of the traits of narcissism and autism are linked, so it's a mistake I won't be making again. With hindsight, it was clear that I was living with a narcissist. Aaron possessed bad boundaries and seemed to be telling me, "You exist to please me, or you do not exist at all."

LEARNING POINTS: YOU ARE NOT RESPONSIBLE FOR SOMEONE ELSE'S ACTIONS

- Narcissists have a strong desire to control the narrative. They may only be interested in the superficial, and they dislike criticism. They constantly put on a false front.
- Everyone deserves a man or a woman worthy of their love. A narcissist will transfer their unresolved emotional baggage onto you, but this is not your responsibility,

and you don't need to claim it. Learn to recognise when you might be feeling misplaced guilt surrounding this. You are not responsible for how someone else is feeling.

- As previously explained, at first, narcissists will go all out with the love bombing. With time, though, their envious nature will begin to take over and they will belittle or look down on the people they perceive as inferior, thus boosting their own ego.
- Most people wish to be the best version of themselves, but a narcissist has an inability or unwillingness to recognise the needs and feelings of others.

13

EVERYONE HAS A BREAKING POINT

OCTOBER 2ND MARKED A YEAR SINCE MY DAD'S passing. I felt so sad, as I longed to be able to talk to him in person, especially given all the struggles I was facing at home. However, I knew in my heart that he was in a much better place – pain free and dancing the jive with my mum in heaven. I used this image of them together to cope with his loss. The difficult first anniversary was made even harder by the fact that Aaron was simultaneously at the peak of his drinking, and I was finding it nigh on impossible to hide this from Charlie. God knows I tried. Aaron would disappear in the morning and wouldn't return until past our dinner time. Charlie and I knew he had been at the pub, but Aaron would never admit it. The most he would say when Charlie confronted him directly was that he'd only had a couple of beers. I didn't know how best to protect the lad. Aaron would often square up to him, while yelling at me, too. At his most inappropriate, he would shout in my face whilst pointing his finger at me and calling me Anne.

"I am not your ex, I am Lovina," I would say.

"You are just as bad as her!" he'd snap. "Money is like water to you, easy come, easy go. You are out of order keeping my children from me."

He would rant about other things that made no sense to me and then go upstairs and start slamming all the doors.

Once, it was so bad that our neighbour called in to ask me if I was OK. They even suggested that I should seek professional help for Aaron. After hearing all the shouting and screaming, they feared for our safety.

"Aaron might be verbally abusive, but he would never physically hurt either of us," I reassured them.

Aaron announced that he was taking part in 'Go Sober for October'. That didn't last long. Maybe a week, max. I found myself dreading evenings in with him, as I knew he would have been down the pub before coming back to the house. He said he was at work, but Charlie and I knew different. On top of that, he would return with a bottle, two bottles or even three bottles of wine. He often wouldn't even try to hide it or would do so badly. For instance, he'd go upstairs to the 'bathroom', even though we had a downstairs loo.

He treated Charlie and me as if we were blind and stupid.

Over time, I arrived at my own breaking point. I truly believe that everyone has that point of no return, and I suggest that you explore what your own might be. Identifying your boundaries from the outset in a relationship may just save your mental health. You will know how much you are willing to take of someone else's inappropriate actions before acting to protect yourself. This is especially important if you find yourself with someone who has an addiction and/or is a narcissist. As I came to learn, protecting yourself is paramount.

Back to my breaking point. Aaron came in looking glassy-eyed, so I asked him where he had been. Dinner had been ready for over two hours and I needed to feed the boy, who was hungry. Aaron rambled on about having a long, overdrawn meeting. Charlie and I looked at each other; we did not buy into it but nor did we say anything. I was truly thankful that Aaron decided to sit with us and eat the meal I had prepared. If anything, it would sober him up. However, as soon as he'd finished, he disappeared upstairs to the bedroom. Twenty minutes or so passed before he came down again, stating that he had been on a work call. At the time, I was busy clearing away dinner. Aaron was slurring as he spoke and was clearly drunk. I had no way of hiding this from Charlie. Half an hour later, Aaron made his excuses again and told us he was going upstairs for a shower.

Once he was out of earshot, Charlie sat down with me and told me that he had been tracking his dad via an app on his phone. He confirmed that Aaron had been in the pub for hours before coming home. I was mortified. It felt like all I had done to try and shield him from his father's alcoholism had been wasted.

Later, I was catching up on some admin, when I heard Charlie screaming at the top of his lungs.

"Lovina, Lovina, Dad's fallen out of the shower."

I raced upstairs to find Charlie standing by the bathroom door. He was staring at Aaron, who was naked in the bath, with his head slumped over the toilet next to it. He appeared to be unconscious. Suddenly, I was struck by a terrible thought. *"Is he dead?"*

I instructed Charlie to go downstairs and get some ice and a tea towel, whilst I checked that Aaron was still breathing before scanning his body for any signs of blood. I deduced that he had hit his head and torso on the toilet basin. Luckily, he hadn't cut himself, but a lump was already visible on his head, along with bruising to his torso. I tried to gently rouse him, whilst reassuring him that he was home, safe and well.

Eventually, he came round, and I placed my arms around him to try and help him up.

"Get off me, you're hurting me!" he screamed out in agony. I realised he could have broken his ribs, but he refused to let me check him over.

"You are a c*nt!" he screamed. "You did this to me. You are evil, just like my ex-wife."

I helped him into the bedroom and lay him on the bed, propping him up with pillows while he continued to shout unnecessary abuse at me, all the time pointing his finger in my face. I decided to check on Charlie and found him on the landing, where he had witnessed everything.

"Leave your dad be," I said gently. "I'll keep checking on him."

As I was talking to Charlie, I could see his attention drawn to something going on behind me. I turned to see a naked Aaron limping out of the bedroom and into the bathroom. It was a sight that neither Charlie or I needed to see, and one that neither of us will ever be able to forget.

Aaron uttered incoherent profanities at us before finally making his way back to bed. I went to try and help him get comfortable, but he refused my assistance and continued to shout at me.

After nearly twenty minutes of this, I left to get him some water and pain relief. On my return, he ramped up the abuse, and it was worse than anything I had heard to date. He was saying that Charlie and I were useless, evil people, and that we were deliberately abandoning him and leaving him in pain. As I approached his side of the bed, so I could give him the painkillers, he began to yell. "You two are the biggest assholes ever. I'd be so much better off without you both."

Then he turned specifically to me and ranted, "Your dad is better off without you, now he's dead! All you want is my money, not me. You are just like her."

Aaron was like a broken record when it came to comparing me to his ex-wife.

This is only a snippet of the stuff he hurled at me that night. I handed him the ibuprofen and paracetamol to take, along with some water to swallow them with, and left the room, closing the door behind me, to shield Charlie and myself from any further abuse.

I felt so protective towards Charlie at that moment, and from then on, he became my number-one priority. He was still developing emotionally and did not need or deserve to witness his role model behaving in this way. I was simply gutted over what had happened.

I decided to get ready for bed, but to make matters worse, when I went to get my dressing gown from our room, I found two empty wine bottles stashed in the wardrobe cupboard. Concluding I couldn't sleep next to Aaron that night, I went downstairs to my home office to pray over what to do next. All I kept thinking about was how Aaron must have secretly downed the two bottles of wine during the twenty minutes or so he was alone upstairs, first while taking a 'work call' and then while having a 'shower'.

I perched on my knees for hours and prayed, taking

my faith to a whole other level, as I passed all my fears, worries and concerns over to Jesus. Not since the loss of my mum and dad had I required so much resilience. And never had I prayed through the night before.

~

Although Aaron regularly reprimanded me for only being after his money, this couldn't have been further from the truth – I had always taken care of my own finances. In fact, in 2007, I set up my own life coaching business from scratch, and I was proud of how it was growing.

I knew from Aaron that his ex-wife hadn't worked, as they had decided she would be a stay-at-home mum. He would go on and on about the money she spent, and how she had her own bank card that he would top up with £1000 every month, to spend how she liked.

As I've said before, I don't judge others and I'm happy that Aaron had this arrangement with his ex, but children or not, I have never been and nor will I ever be a kept woman. It's just not my style. I decided on day one of our relationship that I would always look after myself when it came to money. After Dad's death, the funeral arrangements cost me thousands of pounds, and while Aaron did offer to help me out, I chose to take on the debt myself. This was my dad, and it did not sit well with me to let my boyfriend of only a year pay for everything. This is why the comments

Aaron made regarding money were so unjust. When he spoke out like this, I could genuinely see the signs of his past hurts and childhood trauma. They seemed to be eating away at him deep inside, like a cancer.

From this point on, the dynamics in my relationship with Aaron shifted. He could no longer convince me of anything, and I was no longer prepared to be swayed by his poor judgment of others and his version of past events. The scales had been lifted from my eyes and it continued to hit home – like a huge punch in the face – that the man I had fallen in love with didn't actually exist. Aaron was a fake, an unwell man who lacked both confidence and self-esteem. He was a man who had learned from childhood how to play the victim, and he craved the undivided attention of his loved ones. He hated being criticised, while believing it was OK to constantly reproach others.

My awakening to the real Aaron left me with a heavy heart, as I truly loved him. But while finally facing up to what he was truly like was difficult, I wasn't prepared to put up with his inappropriate behaviour anymore.

LEARNING POINTS: THERE IS NO RIGHT OR WRONG, IT JUST IS!

- In this life, you can't control other people or events, but you *can* control how you react to them. This is a lifelong journey that you must never give up trying to master.

- People with narcissistic personality disorder have trouble handling anything they perceive as criticism.

- Narcissists can become impatient or angry when they don't receive special treatment. During times when you may have put boundaries in place, to protect and preserve your own wellbeing, the narcissist may feel they are lacking that treatment from you, in the form of your undivided attention.

- At times, you may feel that you have wasted too much of your life with a narcissist, especially as they aren't likely to change. But how about choosing to look at all the positives you can take from such a situation? How has it helped you to grow and change?

14

THE ROAD TO RECOVERY BEGINS

THE FOLLOWING DAY, AARON GOT UP AND LEFT FOR work at the crack of dawn. He didn't return home again until late that evening. My apprehension had been building throughout the day and was through the roof when he strolled in dressed in his finest suit and matching Oliver Sweeney shoes. Given the events of the night before, I just didn't know what to expect. He looked as if he was still in physical pain, but to my immense relief, it didn't appear that he had been drinking. He came and sat next to me on the sofa and apologised profusely for his behaviour.

"I've just been to an AA meeting," he explained.

I felt instant relief that my prayers had been answered. I knew this was the beginning of a tough, lifelong journey for Aaron, and it was one that I was more than prepared to accompany him on. The previous night I'd prayed to Jesus for a sign regarding whether to stay with him or not, and I felt like this was it. Had he come home intoxicated, as usual, I would have left there and then.

Deep down, a small part of me wanted the easier option of leaving. However, as best I can, I try to follow the path of faith, so I accepted Aaron's remorse and willingness to change as a signal to stay. Growing up, my mother had always told me, "The difficult road is the right one." What she failed to warn me about was all the painful lessons that would have to be learned along the way. You see, a narcissist will never speak the full truth. They choose which parts of a story to omit, so that later on they can say they never lied. I had to come to terms with this over the years, and to accept that narcissists actually believe their own bullshit. It's perhaps my saving grace that I have an extraordinarily good memory!

With Aaron now in AA, and with my ever-positive nature, I convinced myself that I'd fall back in love with him. I thought that we could return to the relationship we enjoyed at the beginning, before his drunkenness got in the way. Perhaps I was making excuses for him yet again, but I am also a firm believer in giving someone a second chance, especially when they are sick and willing to do the healing work. Aaron had been through a horrendous divorce, and with him choosing to fully give up the drink, I really believed that with time, understanding and patience, our relationship could survive and thrive.

I knew all about healing, as following my reactive depression over the death of my mother, which hit me when I was 24, I'd been doing daily work in order to stay mentally well. This started as soon as I woke, when I took some time out just for me. I'd spend an hour doing some stretching work while listening to worship music. I gave thanks and focused on everything I had, rather than what I lacked. At the end of each day, before going to sleep, I'd unwind and unpack the day. This mostly involved lighting candles, listening to relaxing music and writing lists in my notebook of what I needed to do. I also reflected on my interactions and thought about how I could make changes to become the best version of myself.

Although it was incredibly positive that Aaron had decided to give up alcohol, he wouldn't do the further psychological work required to kickstart the healing process regarding his past traumas. No matter how much I pleaded with him, he refused to have any counselling, and over the course of the coming year, he tried to convince me that the AA programme he was following was enough. But although I was no longer finding empty wine bottles stashed away in cupboards, I didn't witness a more balanced person emerging. Instead, I saw a man with the same cracks that showed when he was drinking. I really had taken the difficult road by choosing to stay and help him work through his alcohol addiction. However, I am not claiming to be a victim and I take full responsibility for deciding to stay with him for the next two years. I will never regret this, as it did help him to remain sober, and I was additionally able to shower his children with the unconditional love they needed. This was especially important for Charlie, as he was taking his GCSEs. Helping him to achieve his goals when everyone else around him believed he would fail was worth all my time and the relentless effort and sacrifice.

During Aaron's first six weeks on the AA program, I watched him really suffer. As he was no longer numbing his pain with alcohol, he was forced to face his past traumas and demons. He attended up to three AA meetings a week, and I was – and still am – incredibly proud of his achievement. Tackling your addiction while simultaneously working through your personal baggage isn't an easy thing to do, but it's a choice you make and then need to stick to. After all, a very wise friend once said to me, "The man at the top of the mountain didn't just fall there!"

But as Aaron embarked on his recovery programme, our relationship suffered. His needs were of paramount importance, sod what I felt. There were nights when he came to bed fully clothed and turned his back on me, pushing me away if I tried to cuddle him from behind. Twelve weeks passed without any affection from him at all. Thanks to the personal healing work I'd done, I didn't necessarily rely on this from him in order to feel loved, but it was hard not to feel rejected.

~

A friend invited Aaron, Charlie and me to spend the Christmas of 2007 at her house. Arabella was spending the day with her mum and was due to join us for Boxing Day. My lovely friend knew that Aaron had embarked on his recovery journey and also sensed that I would be missing my dad. It was nice to feel part of someone else's family Christmas.

When we returned home, Charlie went straight out to meet his mates and Aaron and I settled in for the night. It was actually pleasant to have some quality time alone together. Aaron was in good spirits, and he even thanked me for being there for him. This was probably the last time I can remember him showing me any kind of affection. I am certain it was the last time he whispered in my ear, "I love you, Lovina", with real meaning.

On Boxing Day, Aaron went to pick up Arabella and we enjoyed our 'Family Unit Christmas', as Aaron called it. We sat and opened all our gifts, before watching *Home Alone* while Aaron made our festive dinner with all the trimmings. We had a lovely meal together and enjoyed lots of fun and frolics. When Aaron spoke to his brother, he invited us to spend New

Year in the Lake District with him and his wife and two kids.

"How exciting," I thought to myself. There was going to be eight of us seeing in 2008 in a converted barn. The property had access to many indoor facilities on site, including a swimming pool, an adult spa area, a family gym and a games room, so there would be no chance of Charlie, Arabella and their two cousins getting bored. This would allow the adults to enjoy some quality downtime together. I honestly felt this break was a Godsend, and just what Aaron and I needed to reunite our passion for one another.

LEARNING POINTS: SURVIVING A NARCISSIST

- Loving a man who does not love himself, and in turn will never love you, can be truly painful. Fortunately, the way I was brought up meant I had a solid foundation in life. It was part of my nature to only see the best in my partner, to live in hope and joy, and to try and help him grow, without expecting anything in return. To then be let down by him took its toll. It doesn't matter how mentally balanced you are, loving a narcissist will impact your wellbeing. It is not an easy journey, but you can and will survive it.

- Surviving a narcissist takes time and care on your part. It is important to ask yourself: "Am I mentally balanced and able to cope with them?" If the answer is negative, or even that you're unsure, I strongly recommend some wellness or life coaching. This will enable you to see your worth, to put boundaries in place and to view this chapter of your life as a test of your resilience and unconditional love.
- Narcissists have difficulty regulating their emotions and behaviour. If you can accept and come to terms with this, whilst being able to regulate your own emotions, then you will be able to find some balance.
- If you are balanced and emotionally well in yourself then you should be able to identify when the narcissist in your life is experiencing major problems. These are usually linked with dealing with stress and adapting to change. You can then discuss coping mechanisms with them. If you are able to identify when a narcissist feels depressed and moody, because they fall short of perfection, then you can put preventative measures in place.
- All narcissists carry secret feelings of

shame, humiliation, insecurity and vulnerability. If you can identify and discuss these with them, they may be open to the suggestion of professional intervention in the form of talking therapy. This will enable you to survive your narcissistic relationship without any collateral damage.

15

HOPE

New year, new start? I was truly optimistic about this, given my parents had taught me to live in hope of better things for the future. So, the time had come for us to join Aaron's family for a four-night getaway in the Lake District, and I was filled with excitement about the prospect of our relationship getting back on track. The last two months had been extremely difficult for us both. While Aaron was detoxing, I was on the outside doing whatever needed to help him get through the first stage of his recovery. We had both suffered and endured so much, and I felt we needed some time just for us. Aaron was a different man to the one I had fallen in love with, and I was able to be honest with myself about this. I now wanted the opportunity to get to know the real him. What I failed to understand back then was that I would never come to know the truth of this man. This would only happen if he chose to seek professional help to heal from his past traumas. I loved him, and so I guess I was in denial of the truth that I knew on a deep down, spiritual level. I chose instead to believe that we would get through this and be a strong couple for life. I wanted us to live happily ever after together with his two beautiful cherubs. I still clung onto the hope that one day we might even have a child of our own. Though I could feel the distance developing between us, I continued to believe that our faith in each other would save us, irrespective of the dark times we'd endured.

As if being rewarded for my positivity, we had lots of fun and quality time together in the Lake District. It was nice that Aaron could receive some support from his brother and sister-in-law, as I was emotionally drained and needed outside help to carry him through the initial six months of his recovery programme. Unfortunately, there wasn't the opportunity for us to be intimate, as when bedtime came, all Aaron wanted to do was sleep. Instead of feeling dejected, I looked at the small wins. Aaron was back to grabbing me and bringing me in close for cuddles as I drifted off to sleep. As a result, I slept better than I had done in ages. I felt a sense of peace and truly believed that we may have turned a corner.

The days came filled with fun and frolics. Armed with torches, the children went out on late-night adventures around the property. Of all the cherubs,

Charlie had to be the one to fall into the stream. It was so funny seeing him return to the barn soaked to the skin. He had to strip to his boxers before being allowed inside, which we all laughed about.

The onsite complex had an indoor swimming pool and spa that we were all able to indulge in together. We also enjoyed some beautiful meals and walks. I was slowly feeling Aaron coming back to me, both spiritually and emotionally. The small things always count with me, and I can remember being thankful in my prayers to Jesus for these clear signs of improvement, especially when Aaron held my hand on walks and pulled me into him in bed. These small acts felt like a huge step in the right direction. For the first time in a long time, I felt happy and content, just as I had done when Aaron and I first met in the summer of 2005.

Sadly, a year into his recovery programme, and three years into our relationship, Aaron's true personality began to rear its ugly head once again.

In October 2008, he accepted a new job with a bigger company. This meant he would be commuting a long way and staying away for work during the week. I therefore agreed to support Charlie during his final GCSE year. From here on, my eyes were truly opened to the fact that I had indeed fallen in love with a narcissist. Fast forward to April 2009, a month before my 30th birthday, and Aaron pulled out all the stops to treat me, but in true narcissistic style, this was for show rather than for love.

He booked to take me away to a beautiful 5-star resort in Greece. I did wonder why he'd picked this location. Yes, it was a shorter flight from the UK, meaning it would be easy to get home to Charlie if we needed to, while still enjoying the heat of the sun. However, this was the one time in our four years together that we would be child and responsibility free. In addition, Charlie was due to go away for two weeks with his best mate and his family anyway. So, I couldn't help wondering why Aaron didn't take me somewhere more exotic. I didn't expect anything from him and had never pushed for a marriage or a child, as ultimatums aren't my style. Instead, I had put him and his children first, above my own needs. While I was both happy and appreciative that he had booked us this holiday, I had secretly been hoping we'd visit a place on my bucket list, such as Sicily or Hawaii. Aaron knew how much I longed to visit these places, and yet we went to Greece, which wasn't as special as he'd been there before. He'd also often promised that for my big 3-0 getaway we'd go business class, yet when the time came, he booked us on an early morning budget flight from Gatwick. Looking back, I can see that Aaron had been doing a lot of carrot dangling in order to reel me in emotionally and then keep me. I would have much preferred it had he not made those promises in the first place.

LEARNING POINTS: SEE THE TRUTH BEYOND THE OUTWARD CHARM

- Narcissists love to 'dangle a carrot' or two, in an attempt to control and manipulate a situation. This is designed solely to be of benefit to them. Promises are made and very few are kept. Learning to see the truth, past the charm, is important in gaining some insight into a narcissist's perception.
- Be aware that a narcissist will always insist on having the best of everything, be that a car, home or office.

16

30TH BIRTHDAY YEAR ENVY!

As excited as I was for my 30TH birthday year to commence, I was also coping with the loss of a dear friend and client. This lovely lady, whom I also shared my first name with, had been coming to me for life coaching and healing to help with her terminal cancer diagnosis. We'd connected over our love of Jesus and the angels, and I knew I'd treasure our special bond for the rest of my life. After she passed away on Easter Monday, I had the honour of being invited to her funeral, so I could say my goodbyes alongside her close friends and family. Aaron knew about my connection to this lady, yet he didn't offer to come to the service with me and support me through it. His inaction cut me like a knife. A partnership should be a two-way street, comprising communication, love, patience, kindness and support, yet I didn't seem to be on the receiving end of any of this.

To try and cheer myself up, I decided to do one fun thing a month during my 30th year. Lately, I felt my life had become very routine and dreary. Aaron never wanted to do anything at the weekends beyond the norm. We would spend Saturday daytime ferrying Arabella and Charlie to their clubs, before staying in and watching Netflix in the evening. On Sundays, Arabella, Aaron and I would go to church and after lunch we would all head to the David Lloyd fitness club for a workout. I was desperate to break the routine.

Aaron had a huge chip on his shoulder about my birthday year plans, which to this day I still don't understand. Maybe he didn't like the focus being on me for a change. I vowed to stick to my plan, irrespective of his unkind and unhelpful comments. To kick-start the celebrations, I'd planned a spa retreat with Aaron, and my best mate Kelly had arranged for us to attend a show in Birmingham. When the time came, Aaron was not best pleased about me doing this. He couldn't understand why I had to stay overnight in Birmingham when I could easily drive back home after the show. I explained that Kelly wanted to toast and celebrate my special milestone with me. We'd been friends for over a decade, so she preceded my relationship with Aaron. I wished that he would accept that I had my own life and that everything didn't revolve around him.

When I arrived at the theatre, I was so excited that

I forgot to text Aaron to tell him I had got there safely. I then received some shirty messages from him implying that I'd been lying about meeting up with Kelly for the night. I couldn't see what was so wrong about focusing just on myself for a change. In fact, I'd like to add here that it is never wrong to put yourself first. A narcissist will try and make you feel bad for shifting your attention away from them and onto yourself or others. Because they fear loss and not being good enough, they'll throw their emotional baggage at you when your actions inadvertently rock their equilibrium.

Given that I'm such a sociable person, my close friends weren't impressed by the fact that Aaron hadn't arranged any sort of birthday gathering for my big day. It was my instinct to protect him, so I made the excuse that I hadn't wanted a party. But I felt like I had missed out, so I arranged a meal at a wonderful Italian restaurant. Afterwards, we decamped to the local pub. Aaron decided to take Charlie home, as he was still at a delicate stage of his recovery, which I completely understood.

Admittedly, I was a little tipsy by the time I arrived home in a taxi. Aaron had been texting me while I was at the pub, but I'd been having such a good time that I'd forgotten to check my phone. The front door was double locked, and as I didn't have my full set of keys, I had no choice but to wake him to let me in. He opened the door and didn't say a word before grunting and going back upstairs to bed. In my merry mood, I wanted nothing more than to be loving towards my man. So, I walked into our bedroom, stripped off the jumpsuit I was wearing and jumped into bed. I then started to cuddle up to Aaron, making it crystal clear that I wished to show him some affection. But instead of responding to my advances, he turned around and with both hands rather forcefully pushed me away. He then left the room, while moaning at me for coming to bed drunk.

"How dare you come to bed stinking of booze and without even brushing your teeth," he said. "You have no respect for me – I am in recovery! You are evil!"

Eventually, I must have drifted off to sleep while listening to his repetitive loop of words. At around 5 am, I woke to find myself alone in bed. I was uneasy about Aaron not being beside me, so I went to look for him, finding him in Arabella's small single bed. This just didn't feel right, so I woke him and asked him to come back to our bed.

"Just f**k off, will you, Lovina," he ranted.

Feeling guilty, I sloped off back to our bed. The following morning, Aaron left the house early, without telling me where he was going. It was Charlie who informed me he'd gone to the gym. I texted Aaron to suggest I meet him there, but he didn't reply.

Aaron would never let something go for the sake of peace and harmony. He would hold onto things for hours – even days. When we finally got to speak that evening, he was still fuming. Apparently, he was also upset that I had paid the drinks bill at the restaurant. I always feel slightly embarrassed when the bill comes at the end of the evening and everyone starts to dissect it to work out how much they owe. With this in mind, I chose to take care of the drinks using the deposit I'd already paid to secure the booking. I wanted to treat my friends and it avoided the uncomfortable feeling I usually get. I don't think Aaron was upset about me spending the money, it was because yet again the focus had been shifted away from him.

During the course of our conversation, Aaron accused me of being selfish and unkind for coming to bed stinking of booze while not giving a thought to his recovery.

I reflected on the situation and admitted that I could have handled things better, perhaps by talking things over with Aaron before we went out. I apologised for coming to bed in such a state and went to sit on the sofa. Aaron was walking to the kitchen when he suddenly turned around and came towards me with an angry look on his face. He started pointing his finger at me and shouting over me paying the bill. He didn't like it when I was kind and selfless. He was envious of those who were able to give without expecting anything in return. And when I did something generous, he would get jealous, as my attention and focus were no longer solely focused on massaging his ego.

"If you really have such an issue about money, and me using my own earnings to pay for my friends' drinks, then this is something we really need to discuss," I responded calmly.

My words were met with silence, so I added, "You are just upset that I settled the drinks bill using my own money rather than yours. If you have such a problem with this, how about we talk about you finally putting me on the mortgage?"

I was trying to make a point. Although we lived together, Aaron had prevented me from owning a share of our home.

"Get it into your f**king stupid head that you will never be part of my mortgage," he replied.

"Thanks, Aaron, I'm now clear as to where we both stand."

Aaron was quick to realise how harsh and hurtful he'd been. "What I meant was that right now I can't put you on the mortgage," he said.

But at that moment, I accepted I was just an object to this man, and that our bond was broken. He'd spoken to me with such disrespect that I just couldn't see a way of patching up the cracks between us.

I was to unwittingly unravel even more of Aaron's narcissistic traits during one of his work functions at Royal Ascot.

I can remember the day as if it were yesterday. I woke early to prepare, as given that this was a glamorous work event, I wished to look the part for Aaron. I went the extra mile by hiring a lady to come over at 6 am to do my hair and makeup. Aaron didn't seem overly bothered or happy about this, and I already felt like my efforts were never going to be good enough. However, I lived in hope that the day would be magical and, as it turns out, it was one that I will cherish forever. Regardless of the state of our relationship at the time, I had the opportunity to dress up like a lady and sit in a box not too far from our Queen. Knowing this kind of thing might never happen to me again, I embraced every second of it. My philosophy is that you only get one life so make sure you live it right.

After our arrival, we made our way to the Windsor Garden Box. The glass door leading into it was held open by an impeccably dressed lady with a huge smile. I instantly felt both special and overwhelmed by my surroundings. The round tables were set for fine dining and we were each welcomed with a flute of Moet champagne. Aaron introduced me to some of his team and clients, and it became apparent that I was to be his 'trophy wife' for the day. I realised that my role was to look good and help entertain his clients. Mingling with corporate people while dressed in my finery gave me some insight into a world that I was unaccustomed to.

Following the welcome drinks, we were asked to

take a seat, so we looked around for the name cards indicating where we should sit. The leader of our party came out with his mic to explain the order of the day. He also pointed out that our box overlooked the racecourse on the home stretch, which meant we had a clear view of the finish line. I thought about my dad so much that day, as he used to love his horse racing and putting on five-pound each way bets.

As we tucked into a sumptuous five-course meal, we had our race programmes to hand so we could place our bets whilst eating. Between courses, Aaron left me alone a lot while he mingled with his work colleagues and entertained clients. I thought how it would have been nice of him to check in with his 'sweetie' now and again, but then I remembered that I was no longer this to him.

When Aaron's colleagues asked me what I did for a living they seemed genuinely interested in what I had to say, and they also remarked how pretty I looked. Not once did Aaron comment on my appearance or the effort I'd made to look the part. It made me sad to think I was being taken for granted. I'd dropped everything to buy an outfit to wear and had taken the day off work to accompany him.

Back to the day itself. Despite being a betting novice, I had some lucky wins, which I thank my dad for. I actually felt him by my side that day, guiding me on my five-pound each way bets. I picked out the horses with names that meant something to me. The first horse I backed went by the name of Aurora, which refers to the natural light display in the Earth's sky. It resonated with me because I love stars and had already picked the name out should I ever be blessed with a daughter. The second horse was named Watch Over Me, which was a good fit for my faith in Jesus and the fact that so many of my family members reside in heaven, where I wholeheartedly believe they look out for me. The third and final horse I placed a bet on was called Thanks Be. Well, how could I resist? I had always been truly thankful for everything I have.

Well, Aurora, Watch Over Me and Thanks Be all won their respective races. As none of them were favourites, I walked away with just under a thousand pounds. It was such a blessing, and if you are a person of faith, you will understand it when I say that God gives you what you need, not what you want. And it just so happened that I desperately needed that money to cover some car repairs.

In general, I found it easy to fit in at Royal Ascot. Aaron's work colleagues were a friendly bunch and the majority of them were interested in what I did for a living, as all they knew about was corporate life. I had something different to make small talk about, which seemed to be well received. Rather indiscreetly, one of the ladies even remarked how Aaron was punching above his weight.

By the time we left the venue, my feet were killing me, and I found it nigh-on impossible to walk, so I took my heels off to try and ease the pain. Now, in the past, seeing that I was struggling, Aaron would have offered to carry me, but now he just walked ahead, without offering any help or assistance.

What have we become? I wondered. This wasn't the man I had chosen to be with, the one who would have walked across burning hot coals for me. What had I done so wrong for him to shut down and be so cold and callous?

I was so relieved when we got to the car and I could finally rest my poor, mashed-up feet. During the half-hour journey home, Aaron didn't say a word to me. I felt too uneasy to ask why he was being so quiet and speculated whether it was punishment for something I was unaware of doing.

Back at the house, I turned my focus to heating up the lasagne I'd prepared the night before, as Arabella would be over soon. Meanwhile, Aaron went upstairs to change, coming down two minutes later dressed in only his boxers. Watching me busy in the kitchen, he seemed rather agitated and started incessantly tapping his watch. "What are you doing?" he asked.

"What does it look like I'm doing? I'm putting the dinner on for when you pick up Arabella."

Aaron looked at me in disgust, "We have twenty minutes alone and you choose to spend it in the kitchen," he said.

I realised he meant that we could have been upstairs, having some fun in the bedroom. This would have been a great way to finish off our amazing day, had Aaron once commented on what I looked like or paid any interest in me whatsoever. Had he actually shown me any appreciation for being by his side, I'm sure I would have welcomed his suggestion and jumped into bed with him. Instead, I was flabbergasted.

"Seriously, Aaron, what is going on?" I asked. "You haven't mentioned how I look once today, and you gave me the silent treatment all the way home. Now you expect me to be intimate with you. Am I a prostitute now, because I certainly feel like one?"

Aaron just looked at me with a deadpan expression.

"Is there someone else?" I asked. "You have been incredibly distant with me for the last month."

Aaron ignored me, and then a few minutes later announced, "I am going to get Arabella."

So, that was that. I was left in the dark yet again.

LEARNING POINTS: FROM HERO TO ZERO

- The narcissist in my life went from saying, "I love you, sweetie, you are my world", to, "Fuck off, Lovina, you do my head in." But I had not changed from the kind, giving and sincere lady he had met in the summer of 2005, I had simply exposed his true nature.

When this happens, it is important to keep the balance and realise whose issues are at the forefront – it's always the narcissist's!

- Narcissists never think they're wrong, so they rarely apologise (unless there's something in it for them). They hate to lack control and, metaphorically, like to fight things out. Aaron hated it when I did not fight back and told him how I felt instead. Remember that the less you fight back, the less power you give them.

17

SELF-LOVE, CARE AND BOUNDARIES

IN THE SUMMER OF 2009, CHARLIE HAD HIS FIRST GO karting experience. His excitement was infectious. To my surprise, his mum decided to attend his initial trial at a local track, even when that meant coming face to face with Aaron. I was pleased that she had chosen to come and support him; I am a firm believer in owning your responsibilities. Both Anne and Aaron had decided to have these two beautiful children, so they needed to support them, even if that meant putting their personal differences to one side. This was actually the first time I had witnessed them doing this since Aaron and I had met four years ago. It can't have been easy for Anne, knowing that I would also be present. Little did I know back then how similar our experience of being with Aaron would be. I would come to be discarded, too.

I hope I never have to go through a divorce, but I guess you can never predict whether a couple will stay the course, as people change with time, or else they reveal their true nature, as Aaron had done with me. Whenever Aaron and Anne were in the same room they argued and put each other down, often in front of the children. It was painful to witness, but today at least they seem to have called a truce. I took my hat off to Anne for doing this. In fact, from the position I'm in now, I actually admire her for enduring a decade of marriage to Aaron – I only lasted half that time. I believe she stayed for that long for the sake of her children, and although there are always two sides to any relationship breakdown, I knew what a difficult man Aaron was to live with.

Since Royal Ascot a month earlier, I no longer felt I knew any part of the man I was living with. He was experiencing constant mood swings and either dished out verbal abuse or else totally ignored me. It cut me deep, and I realised that the only one I could take care of in this relationship was myself. Aaron didn't have the capacity to love himself, let alone his other half. There comes a point in your life when you see your own worth and self-love as more important than anything else. This is neither arrogant nor selfish, it is a necessity for survival.

If only Charlie could have spent all his free time go karting. Unfortunately, he had also become mixed up in the drugs scene. With Aaron's business trip to America overlapping my holiday to Turkey, this time to celebrate Kelly's thirtieth birthday, we realised we couldn't leave Charlie home alone. So Aaron decided to take him to the US with him.

I could sense that the boy was fighting his own demons after going through so much trauma both prior to and after his parents' divorce. He now had no interest in his college course and was bunking off to smoke weed. I hoped that the trip to Chicago would help him. He needed to spend some quality time with his dad, and it would also remove him from the temptation of drugs, hopefully helping him to see that he had been making poor choices.

Once home alone, I couldn't settle. Being the spiritual type, I can often sense when a shift in energy occurs. This can make me feel both anxious and uneasy. As it turns out, I had every reason to feel this way.

Arriving back from work one day, I opened the front door and spotted Charlie's cycle helmet on the kitchen worktop. Quick as a flash, I had a prophetic image, as clear as day, of a silver Apple Mac computer covered with lines of white powder. I wondered what to make of it. This kind of vision usually happened while I was listening to worship music, praying, showering or cleaning the house, not after seeing an everyday item on the worktop.

I decided to take some time out to be still, and in the end, I pieced everything together. I was 'seeing' Aaron's laptop with the drug – no doubt cocaine – lined up in rows. Although it wasn't Charlie's computer, I knew he was behind the illegal activity, as I'd experienced the vision after spotting something that belonged to him. I also sensed that the lad was being strongly influenced by whomever had supplied the cocaine.

I needed to deal with the matter, and fast, but with no concrete evidence, I knew I'd sound mad bringing it up. So, I went on Amazon and ordered some Cocaine Detection Wipes, which confirmed what I'd seen.

Not wanting to worry Aaron while he was on his business trip, I decided to raise the matter with Charlie first and give him a chance to explain himself. I messaged him to say that I needed to speak with him urgently, and only when Aaron wasn't around. He called me straight back and I told him what I'd discovered. Taken aback, he then confessed to snorting a few lines with his friends off Aaron's computer.

While I didn't condone Charlie smoking weed, I know that it's often something teenagers experiment with – a passing phase that is mostly harmless. Cocaine, however, was on a whole different level. I knew that if Charlie continued the habit it would affect both his physical and mental health in the long-term. I was also terrified that his dad had taken the computer with him to America. What if he got stopped in customs?

Meanwhile, Charlie was full of remorse over his behaviour, and he begged me not to tell his father about what I'd discovered until they returned to the UK. By this time, I would be in Turkey. After giving it some thought, I agreed with Charlie that I wouldn't speak with his dad until I returned home. This would give him time to reflect and maybe even voluntarily share with his dad what he'd been doing. Charlie also confirmed, to my immense relief, that Aaron hadn't taken the computer overseas with him. Charlie had actually hidden it in the wardrobe so that Aaron wouldn't be tempted to slip it into his hand luggage.

Although I was disappointed by Charlie's behaviour, I can remember feeling overwhelmed and amazed by the powerful pictures that Christ had entrusted me with, so that I could help the boy. I also found this extremely humbling.

I advise all my life coaching clients to regularly take a step back and examine their lives from afar. I believe it's the key to staying balanced physically, mentally, emotionally and spiritually, and it's exactly what I intended to do in Turkey. But first, some fun! Our trip began with an alcohol-fuelled late lunch at the airport before boarding our plane. After landing, we were met by our private taxi, which took us to our home for the week, an apartment belonging to our friends, Stuart and Sarah. They were away and had kindly offered us a free stay in their absence. With Kelly, my partner in crime, by my side to share the experience, I intuitively knew that we were in for a week to remember.

It was late by the time we arrived at the apartment, and we let our sensible sides override our instinct to immediately go out and explore. After all, Turkey would still be there tomorrow. Like two kids excited for Christmas, we settled down to sleep before the fun began. Early next morning, we were up, showered and in search of the Ocean Breeze café. Stuart and Sarah had become good friends with the owner and had entrusted him to look out for us whilst we were on holiday. After a hearty breakfast overlooking the sea and mountains, we decided to spend our first day on sun loungers by the sea, just chilling and catching up.

As the sun began to set, we walked back to our home away from home to get ready for our first night out together in a foreign land. I was looking forward to a few drinks, as out of respect for Aaron's recovery process, I'd stopped drinking at home, and we rarely went out. We hadn't planned to drink much, but once out and about this went straight out of the window. We had our evening meal with a bottle of red wine and then ended up on the upstairs terrace sharing another one, along with a couple of G&Ts, all whilst putting the world to rights. Again, we had the mountains to look out on, and I felt alive and free. My phone died as Aaron incessantly texted me about whether I was home yet. Although we'd stayed out later than we planned, we knew it was time to go home, or else it would spoil the next day. I knew Aaron would be angry that I hadn't contacted him, but since Royal Ascot in June, I was no longer prepared to accept his controlling behaviour. You see, when Aaron wasn't able to reach me, he didn't continuously text out of concern and care, he behaved as if he were my dad, and I was a schoolgirl who'd gone out without permission. I always felt as if I was in trouble with Aaron for simply living my life.

Once I'd charged my phone, I watched in horror as the abusive texts rolled in one after another, beeping their arrival. This put a real damper on the rest of our evening at home, and Kelly ended up taking my phone off me and putting on a Netflix series, which we watched while devouring some snacks. Before bed, Kelly gave me two ibuprofen pills and a pint of water, which she insisted I take to counteract the stonking hangover she was sure I'd have the next day. This is the advantage of going on holiday with someone who likes to party – they know how to bypass a morning headache!

The next day, following a nice lie-in, we headed for the beach, where we enjoyed brunch, before hiring sun loungers for the rest of the day. The resort was such a peaceful place, and I had found a Jojo Moyes novel in the apartment that I wanted to read. Kelly is an avid reader, and I knew I would get bored sunbathing if I didn't have a book to dip my nose into. We spent our second full day in a similar way to the first, reading by the sea and enjoying the peace and quiet. But as the day wore on, we put our books down to chat. Talk soon turned to Aaron and his abusive texts. Kelly encouraged me to take some time out for myself to regroup, rebalance and heal. An hour or so later, my phone began to ring. I ignored it, but then it rang again, and then for a third time. Assuming it was Aaron, Kelly put it out of my reach. But as an overwhelming sadness passed over my soul, I asked her to look at the phone's screen to confirm it was actually Aaron before I continued to ignore the calls. Alas, it wasn't him, it was my friend Holly. I immediately saw a vision of her mother Evelyn and said, "Kelly, I need to answer that call. My mate's mum has just died."

I knew Evelyn as a dedicated, obedient and faithful woman of God, who was loved by many for her kindness and compassion. I called Holly back, who confirmed what I really didn't want to believe – that her mum had passed over. She explained how she had died while on holiday with her husband, Holly's dad. I was in shock from the loss but also because prior to my chat with Holly, Christ had shown me that Evelyn was gone from the physical world. I could feel Holly's pain and grief as she spoke to me, and I consoled her as best I could from afar. My friend knew that I had lost my mother at a young age, so I guess it felt natural for her to talk to me; she knew I would be able to relate to how she was feeling.

I spent the rest of the afternoon in deep reflection. I had seen Evelyn just weeks before her passing, when she had come to sing at my church. Her voice was amazing, like that of an angel praising God. Afterwards, Evelyn, always the caring soul, took the time to ask me how everything was going with Aaron. She said that Christ had shown her images depicting a mountain between us, and that she knew I was suffering emotionally. This happened to be one of the rare occasions when Aaron wasn't at church with me, so Evelyn and I could talk freely. She listened to my concerns over not feeling respected or loved, and she gave me some good motherly advice, telling me that I didn't deserve to be talked down to and belittled. She described what was happening as emotional abuse and prayed for Christ to soften Aaron's heart, and for him to become a man who would cherish and love me for who I am, both inside and out. Evelyn believed that I had given way too much for way too long, and that I had been Aaron's rock during his alcohol abuse, divorce and starting his AA programme.

Sitting on that glorious Turkish beach, I went over and over Evelyn's parting advice and decided that things needed to change in my home life. I was not going to be Aaron's doormat any longer. Throughout our years together, I had served him and his children well, without pressuring him over any of my own hopes and dreams. The time had come to own the truth of the situation and take a leap of faith. I vowed to talk to him as soon as I got home, trusting in God that the outcome would be what I needed, even if it wasn't what I wanted.

During all of my other holidays without Aaron, I had sorely missed him. He was clever at getting deep into my psyche, which meant I felt bad when apart from him for any length of time. However, now I felt different. Evelyn's death reminded me of when my own mother died, and how I'd made the conscious choice to live my life to the full, making decisions that would allow me to become the best version of myself whilst helping rather than hindering others. It was time to embrace this philosophy again.

That evening, rather than letting the sombre mood prevail, Kelly and I spent another splendid evening dining out and soaking up the holiday atmosphere. We toasted Evelyn and the beautiful soul that I had been blessed to cross paths with. The rest of our trip away was both chilled and calm, with no more dramas. We enjoyed the time to ourselves without worrying about our partners, feeding the kids, working full-time and keeping a family home ticking over to our high standards. We loved being in each other's company and everything felt perfect.

LEARNING POINTS: HOW TO PROTECT YOUR OWN SENSE OF SELF

- A narcissist will constantly put you down, until you feel like a dog being beaten by its owner. And if you beat a dog for long enough, it will think it's the norm and won't even run away. Don't allow this to happen to you. Never let someone run you down, belittle you or use what you think or say against you. These are all forms of emotional abuse.
- You may fail to recognise being 'gaslighted' by another, as it may start off with gentle 'teasing' before becoming more constant and nasty. Gaslighting is a form of emotional abuse in the guise of manipulation, and it's a hallmark of narcissism. It may well be friends and/or family that make you aware of the narcissist's inappropriate behaviour towards you. They know you well, so trust their judgement.
- Protect yourself from a narcissist. Do not allow them to distort your reality. They are

very good at blatant lies, spinning the truth
and falsely accusing others. Go with your
gut! If you sense something is wrong,
chances are you are right. Have faith in
yourself and your intuition.

LACK OF EMOTIONAL INTELLIGENCE

FOLLOWING THE TURKEY HOLIDAY, I HAD A LOT OF work on at my life coaching business, so September seemed to speed by. However, 23rd September will forever be imprinted on my heart, as it's the day we celebrated Evelyn's life. I woke up that morning feeling rather glum yet hopeful that Aaron would offer to come with me to her funeral, but he didn't. It truly is an odd feeling when you come to understand that your relationship has run its course, and yet you still love the person you are with. Aaron was not acting as if he was in a partnership with me, and he had shut down when it came to emotions or intimacy.

Evelyn's funeral was an amazing celebration of her life. I felt truly blessed to be there and to listen to all the stories of her younger days, prior to meeting her husband Ken, getting married and having her two beautiful children, Holly and Jamie. It was such a special day, and I would have loved to have had my partner's support. It would have been nice for him to offer to accompany me, and to make sure that I was OK, while paying his respects to my friend's family. Why had I even bothered to hope that Aaron might actually surprise me? After all, I knew him and had already identified his way of working. If it didn't serve him to accompany me, why would he bother? I wasn't prepared to let the constant disappointment change me, though. One of my finer qualities is the hope that I have in others. It can be a cruel thing to be constantly let down, however, I will never – and nor should you – feel the need to change for anyone or anything. Aaron was an unwell man who only ever saw the world from his perspective, but I accepted him for who he was and would never try and change him. In this situation, you learn to either put up or shut up, but in the end, I had to choose self-love. A new path was fast approaching. During Evelyn's funeral, I could feel the winds of change afoot.

These winds arrived a week before Charlie's 17th birthday, but at that moment they were something I neither planned for nor wanted. As my dear mother used to say, when you have to decide on the path to take in life, "There is no right or wrong, it just is!"

It all started on an autumn Saturday. The football final was on the TV, and I was trying to watch it, but the children kept distracting me. All I wanted was to finish watching the game in peace, shower and then go into town to get Charlie's birthday present. Alas, the path I was to take was going to be a very different one.

"Can you take Charlie into town with you, he wants to get a hoodie?" Aaron asked.

I looked at him in disbelief, as he knew full well the purpose of my trip. I had a full work schedule all week, so this was my only opportunity to sort out a gift for him.

"No, I can't, sorry, I have stuff to do," I replied.

Aaron's eyes looked so wild, as if they were going to pop out of their sockets. "Oh, right, you have secret stuff to do, eh? That's why you want to go out on your own."

I couldn't believe Aaron's outburst in front of Charlie and Arabella, especially when he knew exactly what I was planning.

"I am going to shower and then I am going into town *on my own*," I said.

I left the lounge and the game I had longed to watch, just to be away from Aaron's digs. After a long shower, I got dressed and did my hair and make up. Then I went downstairs to discover that Aaron and the kids had gone out.

I called him to ask where he was.

"I've taken the children to town, as you refused to take Charlie with you," he replied.

"That's not what happened, Aaron. You clearly have no respect for me. You just left the house with

Charlie and Arabella without letting me know you were going out or saying goodbye. Why?"

Aaron responded by putting the phone down on me. I decided to go into town as planned, to get Charlie's gift and have some much needed 'me' time. I went to Café Nero and ordered a black Americano, which I drank while working on some blogs for my business. I was deep in writing mode when I heard what I thought was my dad's voice.

"Get the hell out of Dodge, Lovina."

I came over very cold, and then extremely hot, as I sat and wondered whether I was going mad or if I had actually heard my dead dad speaking to me. I prayed on it and asked for guidance while continuing with my work.

"Get the hell out of Dodge."

There it was again.

I turned to the gentleman at the table next to me. "Beg your pardon," I said.

"Sorry, my dear, I didn't say anything," he replied.

Although I couldn't explain what had just happened, I felt the need to go to the home of my pastor Dave and his wife Molly. I needed to be with like-minded people of faith. I left the café and headed to their house, a twenty-minute drive away. When I arrived, Molly opened the door and I immediately felt overcome with emotion.

"I can't go back," I sobbed. "I don't know what to do."

Molly immediately grabbed me and held me tight. I felt safe and at peace. She ushered me into the house, where Dave and I spent some time talking things through and praying. I was guided to text Aaron to explain that I could not come home. I told him where I was and confirmed that I was safe.

"Molly and Dave have said I can stay with them tonight," I wrote. "I didn't know what else to do. We don't ever talk, Aaron. I try and you walk away. I feel so lost and sad right now."

"We're both struggling," Aaron replied. "It all seems to be left to one or two massive chats. I just can't do that and it's really causing us both problems. Are you coming for food?"

"Thanks, but Dave and Molly have cooked for me, as I didn't know how to feel or what to do with myself."

"OK, tough day, and I'm sorry for this. I hope you get some sleep. God bless."

The lack of a loving response from Aaron when I told him I wasn't coming home cut me deep. I felt I was a business transaction, especially when he glazed over what was happening to ask if I was coming for food. That night, while praying in bed, I felt he wanted me gone. Deep down, I knew he would rather I leave than fight for our relationship. For him, things are either black or white, and as I was no longer around to please him, I became non-existent. He didn't try to make amends, instead, he shut me out of his and his children's lives overnight. In a way, by listening to Jesus and going to my pastor's home, I'd given him the easy way out.

Some months later, I found out that he told the children I'd left them. However, truth and light always prevail and both Arabella and Charlie chose to stay in contact with me. A decade on, I am still hearing of their father's repeated narcissistic patterns with his current partner. Many times, I have wondered whether the woman Aaron replaced me with was already in his life when we split. They seemed to get together almost overnight after we separated. Narcissists are known for '*monkey branching*' when it comes to relationships, so I wouldn't be surprised if she was already on the scene. Meanwhile, post the break-up, I decided I needed to let my wounds heal before embarking on another love affair.

Once single, I began to see things more clearly. I realised that over the past five years, I had become a wife and a mother without the ring or the birthing scars. I had given endless amounts of love and time to my partner, only for him to take advantage of my good nature.

In December 2009, I went to Bali, in Indonesia, to heal myself from this toxic partnership. I needed to give myself time and space to reset, realign and recover from the traumatic experience.

In the early hours of the day of my departure, Dave drove me to Heathrow Airport to catch my flight. I can remember feeling numb, and also rather lost over where I was in my life and what I was about to embark on. However, I felt comforted by my faith and the feeling that my recovery would begin as soon as I stepped on that plane.

I've always been a free spirit, but because of how much I loved Aaron, I'd allowed him to put me in a cage. It was only on my holiday to Turkey with Kelly that I realised just how much my wings had been clipped. Luckily, I had come to love myself in the years prior to meeting Aaron, and it was this, along with my strong faith in Christ, that kept me mentally sane both during and after our relationship. Trust me when I say that if I can leave a narcissist then you can, too. Embarking on a life alone after being part of a family unit wasn't easy, especially as I had longed to be part of one ever since my mother had passed away, but it was the right thing to do for my own preservation. And guess what? I survived! And with time, I even began to thrive, too.

LEARNING POINTS: MAKING THE DECISION TO PART WAYS WITH A NARCISSIST

- Once you've served your purpose, a narcissist will toss you aside like a rag doll and erase you from their life. They believe they are the victims in life and when things go wrong, it is purely someone else's doing. This is why many narcissists refuse to be the 'bad guy' who ends a relationship. Instead, they will make your life unbearable until you call it a day, thus keeping their victim status intact.

- A narcissist will dance around you. He or she will never actually define your relationship. In essence, they will expect you to treat them like their partner – so they get the intimate, emotional and sexual benefits – without making any kind of commitment to you. This means they will still be able to keep an eye out for prospective partners (see the final point). It doesn't matter how much you love them, remember that this isn't acceptable behaviour and you deserve better.

- If you choose to leave a narcissist, choose to be OK with it. In itself, the act of leaving will bring with it lots of misplaced guilt.

Remember, they have got into your psyche and it will take a long time to get them out again. Be prepared for them to bounce straight into their next dysfunctional relationship while you're still licking your wounds. Don't let this detract from your self-love and healing.

- When you leave them, the narcissist will panic and place the blame on you, especially if you try to talk to them about the break-up. They may lash out and make it their goal to hurt you as punishment for abandoning them. To save face, they may also bad mouth you to others in your circle.

- A narcissist may certainly 'monkey branch'. This is when someone prepares for a new relationship while already in one. Their decision to quickly move on from you is a ploy to make you feel jealous and unworthy, and to help heal their own dented ego. They won't reflect on why you left or look at their own part in the relationship breakdown. It will feel as if they have simply tossed you aside. Aaron was like this, which made it difficult for me to get over the relationship. Luckily, time really is a healer and after a year, I felt more like my true self and was ready to date again.

EPILOGUE

THE COVID-19 LOCKDOWNS IN 2020 GAVE ME TIME to reflect and write my memoirs. In doing so, I was able to acknowledge that I have truly forgiven and let go of Aaron. I will never regret those years I spent with him, as they taught me so much.

If you are, or have been, in a relationship with a narcissist and have also read my story to completion, you will know that there is always another way to live and always a way out. It is important to remember that the choice over whether to stay or go is in your hands. And I can assure you that if you do choose to leave, you will never entertain, let alone endure, a narcissist again. You will allow only a man (or woman) worthy of your love into your inner circle of trust.

It isn't healthy to dwell on mistakes or what you have gone through in the past. Holding onto negative feelings regarding the narcissist is a waste of time and will drain you of your positive stores of energy. The one thing I could do once I'd left Aaron was to own the part I'd played in our relationship and then move forward with my own healing.

I pray now that these memoirs will help others who have lived through a relationship like mine. For those of you reading this memoir who are still deep within a narcissistic relationship, be it with a partner, family member or close friend, I hope my words give you the courage and strength to survive. Take a deep breath, dear reader, trust in yourself, work on your 'self' and remember that love is the key to healing.

ACKNOWLEDGMENTS

After years of personal suffering, sacrifice, compromise, deception and the endless losses of those closest to me through death, I finally took the time out during the Covid-19 pandemic to relive the emotional moments of my life and write my story, in the hope of helping others.

My first book of many has finally been published, and I truly hope it will help people suffering because of narcissism and/or addiction. I wish to take a moment to thank Jesus for asking me to 'step out', and to pay homage to those friends of mine who truly believed in my crusade.

Printed in Great Britain
by Amazon